A PORTRAIT OF MY FATHER

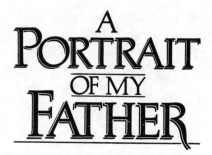

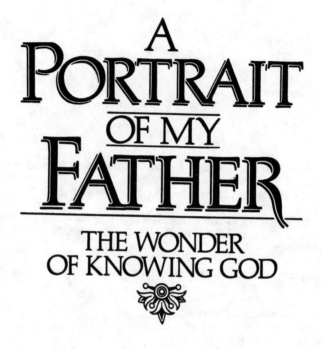

A PORTRAIT OF MY FATHER

THE WONDER OF KNOWING GOD

PETER W. LAW

FOREWORD BY DON BAKER

MULTNOMAH · PRESS

Portland, Oregon 97266

Back cover photo by Louis Bencze
Cover design by Larry Ulmer
Edited by Steve Halliday

A PORTRAIT OF MY FATHER
© 1985 by Multnomah Press
Portland, Oregon 97266

Printed in the United States of America

Library of Congress Cataloging in Publication Data
Law, Peter R., 1950-
  A portrait of my Father.

  Bibliography: p.
  1. God.   2. Spiritual life.   I. Title.
BT102.L39   1985   231'.1   85-15458
ISBN 0-88070-107-2 (pbk.)
85 86 87 88 89 90 — 10 9 8 7 6 5 4 3 2 1

Dedicated to Alexander Walter Law,
whose fatherly example on earth has demonstrated not only grace,
humility, and courage, but above all, commitment
to our Heavenly Father, whose portrait is attempted
in this volume.

CONTENTS

FOREWORD

A portrait is the product of a skilled hand, a ready eye, and a studied gaze. Unlike snapshots that can be secured in but a fleeting moment, portraits require *time*.

Peter Law is well equipped to sketch a word picture of his Heavenly Father. He has known Him from childhood, has studied Him with care, and has sketched with the integrity of a true artist careful to capture every detail of His Person.

Born in Australia, introduced to God from the moment of his first breath, trained in the Scriptures as a child, saved as a youth, and called to reveal God to man before entering his teens, Peter has known no other calling, no other purpose or goal in life than that of preaching the truth of God to the hearts and minds of men.

Upon completing nearly a decade of pastoring in Brisbane, Australia, Peter came to the United States to finish his doctoral studies. It was during this time that he began to stimulate the minds of my people at Hinson Church in Portland, Oregon, with his intimate and detailed glimpses of his Heavenly Father. This ministry became in great demand. His messages always inspired; his life never ceased to challenge.

Peter knows his Father well. And in this day when God is obscured by the lengthening shadows of man, he gives to us a glimpse of Jehovah that is desperately needed and gratefully received.

Don Baker
Pastor, First Evangelical Free Church
Rockford, Illinois

ACKNOWLEDGMENTS

Like most teachers and authors, I am indebted to others. My thinking has been spawned in the many tributaries of other men's thought. For this reason it would be wrong to claim originality for every idea expressed in these pages. I therefore will not make the claim. But it would be equally remiss of me to acknowledge the help of other sources without identifying them.

So little has been written on the Fatherhood of God. Scanning the available material prompts us to travel back to the previous century in order to find the catalyst for modern contributors to this wonderful subject. Recent contributions exhibit one common trait—the influence of the nineteenth-century works by P. T. Forsyth, published again in 1957 by Independent Press of London under the title, *God the Holy Father*.

I, too, am indebted to Forsyth and to the writings of those whose scholarship and insight have added new dimensions to my appreciation of God as Father.

To men like Smail, Bingham, and Packer—to name just three— I say thank you for helping to open up the delights of knowing God as my Father . . . *our Father*.

With appreciation.

INTRODUCTION

BRUSHING UP ON FAMILY PORTRAITS

Have you ever watched an artist at work? Have you stood and wondered at his (or her) ability to push oil around on the canvas in such a way as to convince your eyes that what is taking shape on the easel is in fact a real scene into which you could step?

Of all the artists I admire, the master of portraits heads the list. It intrigues me to watch a "personality" emerge as each new layer of paint builds upon the former until finally, the artist's subject is reproduced before you.

The portrait I will attempt in these pages has already been painted to perfection by another Artist. Our Lord Jesus Christ has produced a stunning portrait of God, but without the aid of oils, brush, or paint. Of course, it would have been impossible for God, who is a Spirit, to be captured in such a way. Rather, Jesus produced that portrait in a single word—a word which envelops so very much because it is so deliberately accurate. An all-encompassing word. A word which paints God with verbal precision. That word is—*Father*.

In 1913, Charles Foster Kent of Yale University had this to say regarding Jesus' portrait of God as Father:

INTRODUCTION

In leading His race back to a simpler, truer conception of God, Jesus expressed the essence of religion in the one all-embracing word, Father. His teaching was the culmination of a process which may be traced from the beginnings of human history.... He gave to the term, father, a reality and a personal content that made his teaching a new message to men. He divested the term of all national limitations and interpreted it universally. He spoke not only of My Father, but of the Father, your Father and our Father, and used these titles interchangeably. The designation assumed ... that it is possible for man to communicate with God and to know Him intimately.... The foundation of Jesus' teachings regarding God, therefore, was the supreme mystery, and yet reality, of human experience: the possibility of man's entering into personal relations with his divine Father.[1]

It is to this same Father and to this potential relationship that every key thought in these pages is pointed. We affirm the Fatherhood of God in a day when confusion reigns as to the true character of the one true and living God. It is in the hope that a knowledge of God the Father will bring forth true worship and deliver comfort to anxious hearts, that these reminders of the Father are given.

This *Portrait of My Father* is "painted" with the prayer and in the hope that all of us might not only understand what is being said about our Heavenly Father, but that we will come to know him and love him in a richer and more personal way.

It is my deep hope that this volume will contribute to the healthy heartbeat of the Father's children in general, and to yours in particular as the reader.

Peter Law

---

1. Charles Foster Kent, *The Life and Teachings of Jesus* (New York: Charles Scribner's Sons, 1913), pp. 137, 138.

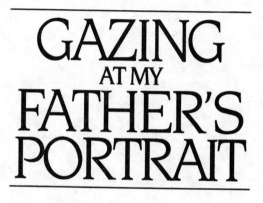

GAZING
AT MY
FATHER'S
PORTRAIT

Isn't He
Like His Picture

"The only sane response all of us can make
is to trust the heart of our heavenly Father,
whose heart is infinitely wise and whose actions
reflect a loving purpose."

1

A PICTURE OF MAJESTY AND MIGHT

Have you ever walked through an art gallery and taken time to stop, peer at a portrait on the wall, and wonder about the personality of the one depicted on canvas? There, suspended before you, is the image of a man or woman whose two-dimensional representation affords you no other information than what you see immortalized in oil. Nothing of this person's character is confirmed by a written description. No one stands next to the portrait claiming to have known the gentleman or lady portrayed. No information is volunteered by the artist apart from what he has told you through his brushwork.

Any conclusions must be left to your imagination. Even the portrait of a well-known historical figure will reveal only so much, and may often suggest a very different character from the one described in history books.

With God, it is very different. He has painted His own portrait. He has left nothing out that is essential to our knowing Him. The portrait is accurate. The color tones are true to life. All characteristics are depicted with precision. While we may not fully comprehend everything about Him, while it may take years of walking and talking with Him to appreciate His ways of thinking and acting, the picture given us is nonetheless complete.

To what portrait do I refer? To that found in the Word of God, to everything which has been written in Scripture, confirmed in His handiwork, and revealed in the life and teaching of God's Son, the Lord Jesus Christ. But one thing needs to be made clear from the outset. We cannot truly study God's portrait without hungering after God. That hunger, in fact, must be the starting point. And there's something exciting about that—to hunger and thirst after God is the same thing as hungering and thirsting after righteousness; and our Lord promised that such hunger will be satisfied (see Matthew 5:6).

The Importance of Thinking about God

Do you spend much time thinking? In the *busy*ness of full schedules it is not easy to find time to think. Many things monopolize our moments: work pressures, family pressures, school pressures. Our days are occupied with demands, expectations, and frustrations.

There seems so little time to sit quietly, to contemplate in peace, or to walk on the beach or in the country. Yet we need to take time to think.

When you do finally get time to think, what do you think about? Life? Happiness? World problems? Holidays? What the future holds? What you will do when you retire? What you will be when you grow up? How to make money in a slumped economy?

What thoughts occupy your mind? Are you a worrier, always doing battle with worry? Do you spend most of your thinking time in worry? The United States Public Health Service printed an article supposedly inspired by the words of our Lord Jesus. This is what the article said:

> So far as is known, no bird ever tried to build more nests than its neighbor. No fox ever fretted because he had only one hole in which to hide. No squirrel ever died of anxiety lest he should not lay aside enough for two winters instead of one, and no dog ever lost any sleep over the fact that he did not have enough bones laid aside for his declining years.[1]

The apostle Paul told the Christians in Philippi that there was no need for anxiety—no need to spend their thinking time in worry. He wrote:

> Finally, brothers, whatever is true, whatever is noble, whatever is right, whatever is pure, whatever is lovely, whatever is admirable—if anything is excellent or praiseworthy—think about such things (Philippians 4:8).

What things are true and noble? Right and pure? Excellent and worthy of praise?

Dr. James Packer, in his book *Knowing God*, quoted C. H. Spurgeon, a man who wrote over a century ago yet whose words are no less true today. Spurgeon wrote:

> The highest science, the loftiest speculation, the mightiest philosophy which can ever engage the attention of a child of God, is the name, the nature, the person, the work, the doings and the existence of the great God whom he calls his Father. . . . No subject of contemplation will tend more to both humble and expand the mind than thoughts of God.[2]

Writing many years later, A. W. Tozer expressed it this way:

> . . . the gravest question before the Church is always God Himself, and the most portentous fact about any man is not what he at a given time may say or do, but what he in his deep heart conceives God to be like.[3]

Thoughts of God like these—thoughts of God my Father—are given birth as I open His Word, the Bible, and as I begin to prayerfully consider who my heavenly Father really is and what He is really like.

As His children we ought to know Him. As members of His family we ought to know what He is like. What I am seeking when I turn to His Word is not merely a verse to dig into, not merely a theological system to think through, but a knowledge of God Himself. I want to know Him. I want to walk hand-in-hand with Him.

My heart is so gladdened when I turn to the Scriptures and realize that it is possible for me to actually know the

One who is behind the words. Our Lord on more than one occasion made that clear. Jesus' prayer to the Father explained the basic elements of eternal life when He prayed: "Now this is eternal life: that they may know you, the only true God, and Jesus Christ, whom you have sent" (John 17:3).

I want to know Him—don't you? I want to walk hand-in-hand with Him—don't you? God Himself has said:

> I love those who love me, and those who seek me find me (Proverbs 8:17).

God spoke through the prophet Jeremiah to His people and said:

> You will seek me and find me when you seek me with all your heart (Jeremiah 29:13).

Through the prophet Isaiah, God spoke a word of challenge to His people to return to Him, saying:

> Seek the LORD while he may be found; call on him while he is near (Isaiah 55:6).

God does not fling snippets of information willy-nilly around the universe as a man may aimlessly throw pebbles into a pond. He does not indiscriminately advertise Himself in hopes that the ripples of divine knowledge might latch onto the minds of men standing in the way. Rather, He reveals Himself purposefully and intentionally.

God reveals Himself through His handiwork in creation. He reveals specifics about Himself through the Holy Spirit's application of God's Word to the hearts of men and women, boys and girls. Paul spoke of the hidden wisdom of God which was no longer hidden from the children of God, but revealed through the Spirit himself, who "searches all things, even the deep things of God" (1 Corinthians 2:10). This "searching" is purposeful. Paul writes:

> For who among men knows the thoughts of a man except the man's spirit within him? In the same way no one knows the thoughts of God except the Spirit of God. We have not received the

spirit of the world but the Spirit who is from God, that we may understand what God has freely given us (1 Corinthians 2:11-12).

Knowing my heavenly Father, His person, His characteristics, His desires for us, and those things "freely given us," is all wrapped up in the parcel of God's purpose for His children. In knowing Him we may glorify Him with our lives and enjoy Him forever as our Father.

When we study God's Word, we study His portrait. But two things need to be remembered: First, as mentioned earlier, we must not separate taking the initial step to study God's portrait in the Scriptures from hungering after God. Second, Packer assures us in his book, *God Has Spoken*: "One of the many divine qualities of the Bible is this, that it does not yield its secrets to the irreverent and censorious."[4] We must embark upon our study of God's portrait with a hunger, with reverence, and without a sense of disapproval at the way God does things.

Have you ever stood and gazed through the glass window of a jeweler's shop and just admired the radiant gems sparkling under the lights? I love to stand with my children and discuss what their choice would be if they were a princess or a king.

When King David blessed the Lord in the sight of all the people, he used words that form a cluster of precious gems which reveal the priceless qualities of our heavenly Father. David said:

> Blessed art Thou, O LORD God of Israel our father, forever and ever. Thine, O LORD, is the greatness and the power and the glory and the victory and the majesty, indeed everything that is in the heavens and the earth; Thine is the dominion, O LORD, and Thou dost exalt Thyself as head over all (1 Chronicles 29:10b-11 NASB).

If our hearts pant after God (Psalm 42:1), we will eagerly turn to His portrait—His Word—as our starting point. But before we open our Bible, we are reminded by the Puritan writer, John Preston, that two things ought to be known about God and recognized as the springboard for such a vast, immense study as this. First, we ought to know *that* He is; and second, we ought to know *what* God is like.

Certainly we must acknowledge that it is impossible to embark upon an honest examination of the character of our heavenly Father without first believing that He *is*. The writer to the Hebrews said, "And without faith it is impossible to please God, because anyone who comes to him must believe that he exists and that he rewards those who earnestly seek him" (Hebrews 11:6).

Once we believe that He is, we must learn what He is like; and to do that, we need to study His self-portrait. In so doing, we will discover the precious gems which cluster in a visible display of His beauty and grace.

I've always thought it very clever how a jeweler/watchmaker can place that little eyeglass between his cheek and eyebrow and hold it there, examining the gems with both hands free to work.

Let us put our eyeglass in place and begin to examine three precious gems concerning God which David marvels over.

Our heavenly Father is majestic and mighty. He is high and lifted up. God is truly His Majesty.

Kings in oriental cultures are often lifted up and borne along on the shoulders of carriers. As they pass by, the people bow and pay homage. But no man on earth can be lifted to the heights of God's majesty. The angels stood before the shepherds heralding the birth of our Savior—a whole host of them, praising God and saying, "Glory to God in the highest!" No man on earth is worthy to be held up as the object of our worship. That belongs exclusively to God. The Psalmist writes, "To *you* O LORD, I lift up my soul" (Psalm 25:1).

Many civilizations and many citizens of earth throughout history have considered themselves mightier than God. The Egyptians fought against God and lost—their doom was sealed when the Red Sea crashed down upon their horsemen. Alexander the Great trekked across the map, conquering wherever he went—but his kingdom too collapsed. Napoleon and Hitler raised themselves up and made quite an impression for a time—but that, too, was short-lived.

Nebuchadnezzar set himself up as the object of men's worship—and God stripped him of every human vesture. He lost his sovereignty and his kingdom; he lost his home and his dignity; he became like an animal; and only when he humbly raised his eyes to God, praising and honoring the Most High, true Sovereign of heaven and earth—only then did God restore him as king over Babylon. He came to see that he could never challenge God's position as sovereign ruler—nor His majesty as king.

One of the Puritan writers put it this way. He said: "One Almighty is more than all mighties." God Almighty is mightier than the most forbidding forces roused by men: mightier than the dollar; mightier than the San Francisco 49ers; mightier than Washington, D. C.; mightier than the Kremlin; mightier than all man-made might which crumbles before the strength of our eternal God.

What is the result of recognizing God's true position as the Almighty, the Majestic One, high and lifted up? It is like Gideon's, a man who witnessed the triumph of God against the Midianites despite the fact that God had whittled Gideon's army down from 32,000 men to a mere 300—*we bow in worship* (Judges 7:9a-21).

The Psalmist beckons us: "Come, let us bow down in worship, let us kneel before the LORD our Maker; for he is our God . . . " (Psalm 95:6-7a). His call summons us to humble ourselves before God in worship. Gideon bowed in worship when he recognized that it was God's power that won the battle against the Midianites. God wanted Gideon to use only 300 men. Why? Because Gideon might otherwise have thought of it as his own victory.

It is so easy to cry to God in times of trouble, but later, when the problem has been solved, to boast that "It was my power that delivered me!" forgetting that it was God who intervened.

We recognize the majesty of God in at least two ways: (1) We are challenged to acknowledge His greatness; (2) we are called to bow in worship (and no man or woman is exempted).

When Queen Victoria of England had just ascended her throne to become Monarch of England, she attended, as was customary for the royal family, a performance of the *Messiah*.

She had been instructed not to stand during the singing of the "Hallelujah Chorus" like everyone else, but to remain in her seat. As the chorus of voices broke into the line, "Hallelujah, Hallelujah, for the Lord our God the omnipotent reigneth," she reluctantly held her sitting position; but as they burst forth in the chorus to acknowledge Christ as "King of kings," the young queen stood to her feet, head bowed in recognition of the greatness of God and her place as a worshiper at His feet.

All earthly crowns surrender before the Monarch of heaven and earth, His Majesty, the King of kings, our heavenly Father.

Our heavenly Father is majestic and mighty in creation. A heathen philosopher once asked, "Where is God?" The Christian at his side replied, "Let me first ask you, 'Where is He not?'" Look around you and see the stamp, the sign, the imprint of the living God (see Romans 11:36; Acts 17:22f.), and remember that the same God whose signature is stamped on creation is the Christian's heavenly Father.

God is truly *His Majesty*. David repeats the theme in one of his Psalms. He writes, "O LORD, our Lord, how majestic is your name in all the earth! You have set your glory above the heavens" (Psalm 8:1).

When you think of a king and his majestic splendor, you think of gilded thrones like that of the boy king, Tutankhamen, you think of lush red carpets, together with a crown studded with precious stones. But the living God has no need of such trivialities to display His majesty. "O LORD, our Lord, how majestic is your name in all the earth!" Our heavenly Father's splendor is everywhere—all over the earth. It cannot be contained—not even by the furthest-flung boundary of space.

Have you ever stood on the precipice of a gorge and

looked over, watching as the water plummets thousands of feet under the force of gravity until it smashes into the rocks below—without crying within you, "O LORD, how majestic is Your name in all the earth!"

Have you ever stood on the top of a mountain range and looked out across the endless peaks, standing proudly in their snow-white shawls, without taking a deep breath— and crying out in your spirit or at the top of your voice, "O LORD my God, how majestic is Your name! O God, how great You are!"

A trip to the planetarium is one thing; but it lacks the majesty of the creation. Replace it with a trip into the wilderness and sit back at night to watch the majesty of our God go through its paces before your very eyes. See His majesty in other ways: watching in wonder, awe, and praise as a tiny baby enters the world. To hear the sounds of silence at night or the crashing of waves against the face of a cliff. All this helps to gain a right perspective on the world which reflects our Father's majesty.

My personal perspective changed the first time I flew in a jet plane and looked out to see the vastness of what God has made. When we crossed the waters that divided Australia from other countries of the world—to be suspended forty thousand feet above the earth's surface in a sea of blueness—that was truly awesome!

I remember one of our daughters was struck with amazement that we could be suspended so far above the ground. She expressed it the best way a five-year-old could. She called to me across the aisle of the plane, "Daddy, look! The plane's wings are not even flapping!" And if it is amazing that by the power of a jet engine we could be propelled in mid-air, how much more amazing that our heavenly Father put the stars in place and the planets in orbit, and that by His power it all hangs together in perfect order!

It was this truth which so activated the mind of scientist Werner Von Braun, who played a significant role in space exploration. It was this truth that led to his salvation. He read in Colossians:

> For by him all things were created: things in
> heaven and on earth, visible and invisible,
> whether thrones or powers or rulers or au-
> thorities; all things were created by him and for
> him. He is before all things, and in him all things
> hold together (Colossians 1:16,17).

God created all that there is from nothing. He created
by His Word (Genesis 1:1f.). Look out at the sky tonight, or
on a clear night, and remember that your heavenly Father
holds it in place so that it does not tumble down on top of
you. Men hurl their satellites into space; but their powers
are so limited that space keeps spitting their tons of iron
back onto the surface of the earth. But when God puts the
stars in place, they stay there by the word of His power.

I love the authoritative statement of Genesis 1:1, "In
the beginning God created the heavens and the earth," and
in verse 3 "God said, 'Let there be light' and there was
light"! How very beautiful! How very powerful! The earth
had a beginning and our God was there! *That* is our
heavenly Father. God saw that creation was good, good for
His glory; it was good for the apex of His creation, for men;
good for you and for me; good to place men and women in
it so that He might love them and relate to them. How sad
that sin spoiled that relationship. How wonderful our
Father's grace that He should send the Lord Jesus Christ to
die to restore lost sinners who turn their back on sin and
worship the living God!

Our heavenly Father is majestic and mighty through time. He is
eternal and unchanging. The Psalmist tells us, "you have
uprooted their cities; even the memory of them has
perished. The LORD reigns forever; he has established his
throne for judgment" (Psalm 9:6b-7a).

You become tired, and so do I. You grow weary in the
tasks of life, in the pressures, the demands, the responsibilities—and so do I. You grow weak in the Christian life
with all the flirtations of ungodliness that bear down on
you from all angles and sides, and so do I. Your nerves become exposed and you feel so weak. And so do I.

As a young boy I loved to spend time on a friend's

sheep station at weekends and on holidays. One of the things we liked to do was to swim in a large natural dam, a marvelous thing since the coast was 120 miles away. One afternoon, at the beginning of a weekend, we were swimming together in the dam. Each of us had a hard plastic kickboard and we would sit on them, holding them under the water, out in the middle of the dam.

Suddenly my float flew out from under me, skimmed across the top of the water, hit my friend's float, and bounced back, hitting me in the mouth. I knew immediately what had happened. The impact had broken my tooth clean in half. I knew, because the nerve was exposed and dangling! Every time I breathed in, a force of air would blast across the nerve. It was painful! I remained like that, unable to get to a dentist for several days.

Life can have that effect on us. It can leave our nerves raw and exposed.

When I am at my weakest point, I need to know the strength of my heavenly Father. Then I am weak, and I know it. When I recognize my frailty, it is good to know that my heavenly Father is eternal and strong—not subjected to fatigue or to wearing out.

Isaiah asks us, "Do you not know? Have you not heard? The LORD is the everlasting God, the Creator of the ends of the earth. He will not grow tired or weary" (Isaiah 40:28a). Rather, "He gives strength to the weary;" to those who grow weary in his service, who grow weary in the pursuit of godliness when the pressures of the world are so great.

We may employ our time in pursuit of many things: academic goals, ambitions, business ventures—and grow weary as a result. But that is not what Isaiah talks about in this passage. He speaks of someone losing heart. In the face of everything opposed to God our eternal heavenly Father, we may have confidence in His enduring strength. Jesus' endurance—the Son of God's endurance—is foundational to ours:

> Therefore, since we are surrounded by such a great cloud of witnesses, let us throw off everything that hinders and the sin that so easily

entangles, and let us run with perseverance the race marked out for us. Let us fix our eyes on Jesus, the author and perfecter of our faith, who for the joy set before him endured the cross, scorning its shame, and sat down at the right hand of the throne of God. Consider him who endured such opposition from sinful men, so that you will not grow weary and lose heart (Hebrews 12:1- 3).

Isaiah comes with sustaining words of encouragement from God for that person whose nerves are raw in the service of the living God:

Though youths grow weary and tired, and vigorous young men stumble badly, yet those who wait for the LORD will gain new strength; they will mount up with wings like eagles, they will run and not get tired, they will walk and not become weary (Isaiah 40:30, 31 NASB).

If your heavenly Father never grows weary, then you may have confidence in times of weakness that He is the source of your strength.

The fact that God is eternal and the eternal source of the Christian's strength has very practical applications for the parent in pain who longs for his or her child to embrace the example of Christian faith set by the parents over many years; for the teenager who daily faces the struggles associated with standing for Christian principles in high school; for the factory worker who is regularly confronted with challenges to his faith; for the doctor and the nurse who stand firmly against the excesses of medicine in relation to human life; for the businessman who stands for honesty in every transaction.

Growing weary in the pursuit of godliness drives the child of God to the Father's embrace. If we change with moods, it is a sign of our immaturity, our inconsistency. If our heavenly Father changed—strong one minute and weak the next—we could never have confidence in His power to strengthen us, whether by His actions or by His Word. But as God Himself spoke through the prophet Malachi, so we trust—for He said, "For I, the LORD, do not change; therefore you, O sons of Jacob, are not consumed" (Malachi 3:6 NASB).

William Tyndale, who had been imprisoned for his part in translating the Scriptures into English and who was eventually martyred, wrote from his damp cell at Vilvoorde (1535-1536), during the last winter of his life, a letter which is believed to have been addressed to the Marquis of Bergen:

> I believe, right worshipful, that you are not aware of what may have been determined concerning me. Wherefore I beg your lordship, and that by the Lord Jesus, that if I am to remain here through the winter, you will request the commissary to have the kindness to send me, from the goods of mine which he has, a warmer cap, for I suffer greatly from cold in the head, and am afflicted by a perpetual catarrh, which is much increased in this cell; a warmer coat also, for this which I have is very thin; a piece of cloth, too, to patch my leggings. My overcoat is worn out; my shirts also are worn out. He has a woolen shirt, if he will be good enough to send it. I have also with him leggings of thicker cloth to put on above; he has also warmer night-caps. And I ask to be allowed to have a lamp in the evening; it is indeed wearisome sitting alone in the dark. But most of all I beg and beseech your clemency to be urgent to the commissary, that he will kindly permit me to have the Hebrew Bible, Hebrew grammar and Hebrew dictionary that I may pass the time in that study. In return may you obtain what you most desire, so only that it be for the salvation of your soul. But if any other decision has been taken concerning me, to be carried out before winter, I will be patient, abiding the will

of God, to the glory of the grace of my Lord Jesus Christ, whose Spirit (I pray) may ever direct your heart. Amen. W. *Tindalus*[5]

Though weary, this man of God left us a testimony to his experience of the sustaining strength of God's Word to him throughout his life. He longed for the Scriptures. Even if his requests for physical warmth were refused, he wanted the assurance that he would have access to his heavenly Father's words, no matter what. They would sustain him.

Shout for joy to the LORD, all the earth. Serve the Lord with gladness; come before him with joyful songs. Know that the LORD is God. It is he who made us, and we are his; we are his people, the sheep of his pasture. Enter his gates with thanksgiving and his courts with praise; give thanks to him and praise his name. For the LORD is good and his love endures forever; his faithfulness continues through all generations (Psalm 100).

The challenge of God's Word to us today is to bow in worship before our heavenly Father—the true and living God.

Come, let us bow down in worship, let us kneel before the LORD our Maker; for he is our God and we are the people of his pasture, the flock under his care (Psalm 95:6,7).

Frederick Faber wrote of God our Father:

Only to sit and think of God,
Oh what joy it is!
To think the thought, to breathe the name;
Earth has no higher bliss.
Father of Jesus, Love's reward!
What rapture it will be,
Prostrate before Thy throne to lie,
And gaze and gaze on Thee!

1. Cited by C. E. Macartney in *Macartney's Illustrations* (New York: Abingdon Press, 1945), p. 414.

2. J. I. Packer, *Knowing God* (Downers Grove: InterVarsity Press, 1973), p. 13.

3. A. W. Tozer, *The Knowledge of the Holy* (New York: Harper & Row Publishers, 1961), p. 7.

4. J. I. Packer, *The God Who Has Spoken* (Downers Grove: InterVarsity Press, 1979), p. 41.

5. D. Edmond Hiebert, *An Introduction to the New Testament, vol. 2: The Pauline Epistles* (Chicago: Moody Press, 1954), p. 358.

2

A PICTURE
OF WISDOM
AND PURPOSE

Don't we usually admire the wisdom of those who come to us for advice? Yet, next to God, we do not have that much wisdom, do we? In his letter to the church in Rome, Paul wrote a beautiful doxology. He expressed it this way:

> Oh, the depth of the riches of the wisdom and knowledge of God! How unsearchable his judgments, and his paths beyond tracing out! (Romans 11:33)

Then, borrowing from Isaiah, he says, "Who has known the mind of the Lord? Or who has been his counselor?" (v. 34).

No, when it comes to wisdom, ours does not compare with God's: "'For my thoughts are not your thoughts, neither are your ways my ways,' declares the Lord" (Isaiah 55:8).

A young man sat in a chair opposite mine. His Mexican features relaxed as he anticipated my reply. But how could I respond? I had just been bombarded by a frightfully heavy load of facts. His eyes closed slightly as if in sympathy with his face muscles, to produce a warm smile. That same smile expressed his recognition that what he had just related was, to say the least, very disturbing.

This well-educated man, Mexican by bloodline, American by birth, and missionary pastor by occupation, had entered my life from nowhere. Now he sat in my presence, describing the horrific experiences his family had endured in the preceding months. The scene? El Salvador. The offenders? Rebel forces. The result? Instant squashing of that which had taken years to establish.

This pastor had been thrown into prison, his wife and children incarcerated. When finally they were released, it was with attached conditions. They must leave the country. Immediately.

En route to the border they were stopped by rebel soldiers. Twice. On the second occasion, soldiers confiscated all their possessions except for a suitcase and some items of clothing. They lost car, watches, jewelry—anything of worth. With their lives as their only remaining valuables, this little family of four set out on foot for the Guatemalan border, ten miles away. In time and with the assistance of many people, they made their way to the United States.

Sitting before me was a man who had nothing to call his own, as the world measures things. No food. Very little clothing. Penniless in a strange place. A modern day "Oliver," only with three dependents—a wife who had grown ill through the ordeal and two little children needing the security of home.

What could I say? How should I respond? Is there an appropriate thing to say? An immediate response might have been to clasp head in hands, to question God's wisdom in allowing such things to happen to His children. After all, "it just doesn't seem right to me that God's family should suffer that way." It is so hard to identify any good purpose in it all. From where I sat, it created frustration . . . especially since I felt so totally helpless in coming to the substantial aid of a stricken family such as this one. But certainly the body of believers would rally together. Help would be found! The dust from the dilemma would settle—but that could never erase what had happened, nor to whom it happened. These are God's own children!

As we sat talking, one thing was obvious. This man loved his heavenly Father. He had no doubts about the Father's love for him. There was no question in his mind that God was in control. He harbored no bitterness toward the Father. The words of Paul to the Corinthian church kept echoing in my mind as I studied this servant of God before me:

> But we have this treasure in jars of clay to show that this all-surpassing power is from God and not from us. We are hard pressed on every side, but not crushed; perplexed, but not in despair; persecuted, but not abandoned; struck down, but not destroyed. We always carry around in our body the death of Jesus, so that the life of Jesus may also be revealed in our body.... For our light and momentary troubles are achieving for us an eternal glory that far outweighs them all. So we fix our eyes not on what is seen, but on what is unseen. For what is seen is temporary, but what is unseen is eternal (2 Corinthians 4:7-10,17,18).

The apostle had faced these things. He knew what it meant to have the carpet pulled from under his ministry's feet. That's why he could write to the church in Rome that most beautiful of doxologies, a statement of praise to God: "Oh, the depth of the riches of the wisdom and knowledge of God! How unsearchable his judgments, and his paths beyond tracing out!"

Well then, am I to become God's advisor? Is it my role to counsel Him? Can I not trust His wisdom on this man's behalf? Among the Hebrew people, the heart was thought to be the location for wisdom. That is why Job said of God, "He is wise in heart" (Job 9:4 KJV).

Our only response must echo Job's. We must trust the heart of God our Father, whose heart is infinitely wise. Job did not try to become God's advisor or to give Him counsel. No, Job's attitude was simple and steadfast in the midst of his trials: "God is wise in heart."

The only sane response all of us can make is to trust the heart of our heavenly Father, whose heart is infinitely wise, and whose actions reflect a loving purpose.

When Wisdom Looks Foolish

Recognizing God's wisdom is not always easy for those of us who are so frequently foolish. Nevertheless, His wisdom will be made clear when we gain a little "inside information." Packer helps us here when he says, "We cannot recognize God's wisdom, unless we know the end for which He is working."[1]

In other words, God has a purpose in mind every time He allows circumstances to give the impression that our whole world is awry. The world looks at the happenings which surround a Christian's life and laughs at the foolishness of faith. The world looks at the claims made by Scripture and sneers, "There is no God." But the Psalmist calls such people fools (Psalm 14:1).

Why does the world come to such foolish conclusions? Because the wisdom of God appears as nonsense in their eyes. You see, if you have tried to ignore God, preferring to worship your own ideas, ambitions, and desires; if you have refused to acknowledge God as your heavenly Father; if you have rejected the Son of God as the visible sign of the Father's love and the means of restoration to God's original purpose in creating you—to love Him, honor Him, and glorify Him in your life—then it is convenient to interpret God's actions as ridiculous.

Turning to the Scriptures, you ask, "Where was the wisdom of God in dealing with Jacob?" (see Genesis 27-35). Jacob the supplanter—the swindler! A man described in modern terms as "a self-willed mother's boy, blessed (or cursed) with all the opportunist instincts and amoral ruthlessness of the go-getting businessman."[2] Jacob, a man who was prepared to swindle his own father and brother for his own ends. Jacob, a man whose nervous potential extended to telling God that if He would fulfill Jacob's desires, then Jacob would allow Yahweh to be his God!

What an arrogant, pompous son Isaac had fathered. Surely Esau, Jacob's twin brother, deserved to be God's instrument, not Jacob. But the Word of God resounds down the corridors of history, declaring, "Jacob I loved, but Esau

I hated" (Romans 9:13). Where is the wisdom in that? Has God made a mistake? Jacob was a "lemon"! Why get associated with him?

God had a purpose in mind. He would take this smooth operator, cut him down to size, and use him for God's glory. Over a stretch of twenty years, God allowed Jacob to dance a "maypole" that would get him into a knotted mess. The strands of deceit and cover-up would produce in his ears a "sin-drone" to which he would have to dance. And it would not cease, it would never stop . . . until he had reaped the sour consequences in his own lifestyle: suspicion of the motives of others, destroyed friendships, dark fears. The kinds of things which drive a person into seclusion for self-preservation, always hounded by the thought that one day someone will see through the deception.

But Jacob failed to take God into account.

God was watching. God was waiting—and all the while He was working out His purposes. What is more, God even allowed Jacob to experience how it felt to be deceived by putting him in the employment of his father-in-law, Laban. That is where Jacob got back some of "his own." Laban was a good match for Jacob. They were equally deceptive, and the pain of poetic justice struck hard.

Finally, Jacob found himself fleeing from his father-in-law even as he faced the prospect of meeting Esau head-on. This was the very same Esau he had cheated twenty years earlier, a brother into whose eyes Jacob had not looked during all that time. A fearful prospect when your heart is beating to a rhythm of guilt! To lock eyes with one you have badly hurt is a confrontation few relish. But God usually requires it—and Jacob was no exception. God wanted to level the deceiver. He wanted to reduce Jacob from a proud con man to a humble, trustworthy man, hating his own dishonest way of life.

This unscrupulous twin stood at night by the river Jabbock. Caught in a trap! Sandwiched between his brother Esau and his father-in-law Laban. Fleeing both! God wanted to break Jacob down. He wanted to bring Jacob to the place of self-distrust. He wanted to disclose Jacob to himself. So God weakened him. God humbled him. And when Jacob's spirit was finally tuned in to God's, God gave him peace.

Jacob became Israel, and from his sons were to come the twelve tribes of Israel. We wouldn't plan it that way! But "Oh, the depth of the riches of the wisdom and knowledge of God! How unsearchable his judgments, and his paths beyond tracing out!"

"For the foolishness of God is wiser than man's wisdom, and the weakness of God is stronger than man's strength," Paul said in 1 Corinthians 1:25. "We cannot recognize God's wisdom, unless we know the end for which He is working," Packer says.[3] Our heavenly Father's wisdom and purpose can be seen through His acts in creation, history, and redemption.

God's Wisdom and Purpose Seen in Creation

Have you ever considered God's wisdom in creation? Everywhere we look, miracles of wisdom flood our sight. "How many are your works, O LORD! In wisdom you made them all." So said the Psalmist (Psalm 104:24). There was divine wisdom in marshaling everything in the universe in its proper place and sphere. How chaotic it would be if the planets and stars could travel about like so many marbles spilled on the sidewalk, thumping and bumping into each other without discernible order!

The universe reflects the glory of God and brings Him glory. You only need to be a hard worker to recognize the wisdom of day and night. The farmer sees the wisdom of the seasons which allows for planting, growing, ripening, and harvesting the crop. Imagine the chaos if all the work had to be accomplished in one season, or if the fruit ripened before it grew!

The wisdom of land and sea—how monotonous it would be if it were all land! If it were all land, those of us who snorkel would find it rather hard going! If all sea, those of us who ski on the mountains would get ourselves into deep water just trying!

The wisdom of families. The interdependence between

one another. Avenues for mutual self-giving and learning to love and serve.

The wisdom of food chains which help to keep the ecological balance of nature. All so wise—and all the creative handiwork of our heavenly Father. Its purpose? For God's glory and for man's good.

God's Wisdom and Purpose Seen in History

In what ways have we seen God at work in history? Let's think of some of them:

(1) Gideon's 300 men (Judges 7:5-15). What? Fight a multitude with 300 warriors?

(2) The healing of Naaman (2 Kings 5:10). What? Washing in the muddy Jordan River to cure leprosy?

(3) The feeding of Elijah (1 Kings 17). What? A poor widow asked to use up all the food she had left in the house to feed a prophet she barely knew?

(4) The bronze serpent on a pole in the desert (Numbers 21:1-9). What? Be cured of deadly snakebites (brought on by disobedience in the first place) by gazing upon a bronze serpent suspended high above the desert floor?

That seems so . . . foolish! In each of these incidents, God's acts appear so oddball! But on the contrary: The more ridiculous the instrument of cure, the more vividly the power of God is seen. And the more clearly the wisdom of God appears!

The plagues of Egypt are another example (Exodus 8ff.). The people of God were in Egypt, under the oppression and affliction of their Egyptian taskmasters. God's way of delivering His people involved plagues. Was that wise? Was that safe? Weren't many innocent people involved? Plagues seem a bit harsh!

Let's examine it for a moment: Each of the plagues of Egypt, which God brought upon the land, was associated with the pagan worship of the Egyptians! They worshiped the Nile-god Hápi. They worshiped Heqit, goddess of fruitfulness, of whom frogs were the symbol. They worshiped the sun-god, Ré, and so on. The Nile—Egypt's god of prosperity—turned to blood and brought ruin; millions of dead and stinking frogs brought disease and waste instead of fruitfulness; the sun was blotted out; the hail and rain heralded awesome events.[4]

Do you see the wisdom of God in the plagues He sent? God took the objects of Egyptian worship and turned them upon the Egyptian people. He took their deities and used them against these Egyptian worshipers in plague proportions. He destroyed the power of the people's gods before their very eyes and declared by His actions, "I am the LORD; that is my name! I will not give my glory to another or my praise to idols" (Isaiah 42:8).

You see, the more seemingly ridiculous the remedy, the more powerful God is seen to be. Isn't He wise! And each of these apparently foolish incidents in history points to the redemptive plan of God! We cannot recognize God's wisdom unless we understand the end for which He is working.

And that brings us to the third aspect for consideration regarding God's wisdom and purpose.

God's Wisdom and Purpose Seen in Redemption

Running throughout the Old and New Testaments is that golden thread which, when woven into the fabric of historical understanding, reveals the purpose of God for His people.

It is that purpose which was spelled out on the day of Pentecost when they marveled at what was preached, crying out: "We hear them declaring the wonders of God in our own tongues!" (Acts 2:11). It is that purpose which Jesus spelled out to the unsuspecting two disciples on the road to Emmaus when, "beginning with Moses and all the Prophets, he explained to them what was said in all the Scriptures concerning himself" (Luke 24:27).

It is that purpose which the Holy Spirit teaches and reveals to the Church when, in the words of Paul, He searches all things, even the depths of God, and reveals them to the believer's heart (1 Corinthians 2:10f.).

In the Cross of Calvary, we see a masterpiece of divine wisdom: foolishness to those who are perishing, but power (and wisdom) to those who are being saved. The world says, "What? How can we live through one who died? How can we be blessed through one who was made a curse? How can we be accepted through one who is condemned?" The Jews said, "What? A crucified Messiah? Ridiculous! A contradiction in terms." Jesus told them:

> You diligently study the Scriptures because you think that by them you possess eternal life. These are the Scriptures that testify about me, yet you refuse to come to me to have life (John 5:39,40).

Paul writes, "Jews demand miraculous signs and Greeks look for wisdom, but we preach Christ crucified: a stumbling block to Jews and foolishness to Gentiles" (1 Corinthians 1:22). The wisdom of God is diametrically opposed to the false wisdom of men.

The center of Paul's message is the Cross—and therefore the sacrificial death of the Messiah. Yet in the face of men's disbelief, men's scoffing and laughter, Paul could write:

> I am not ashamed of the gospel, because it is the power of God for the salvation of everyone who believes: first for the Jew, then for the Gentile (Romans 1:16).

Hodge wrote, "The things which elevate man in the world— knowledge, influence, rank—are not the things which lead to God and salvation."[5] It was never the intention of God that men should come to a knowledge of Him through the exercise of their own wisdom. If God's "foolishness" has brought salvation, how much more will man's "wisdom" bring condemnation and judgment?

The wisdom of God has been summed up in Jesus Christ, the cross of Calvary and His resurrection! Edwards wrote, "God puts His people in the possession of salvation which is at once the mightiest miracle in the guise of weakness, and the highest wisdom in the guise of folly."[6] Before ever you can admire the infinite wisdom of the gospel, you must experience its saving power.

Paul wrote to the Christians in Colossae:

... that they may be encouraged in heart and united in love, so that they may have the full riches of complete understanding, in order that they may know the mystery of God, namely, Christ, in whom are hidden all the treasures of wisdom and knowledge (Colossians 2:2,3)

Well then, is there any room for boasting? Paul tells us:

It is because of him that you are in Christ Jesus, who has become for us wisdom from God—that is, our righteousness, holiness and redemption. Therefore, as it is written: "Let him who boasts boast in the Lord" (1 Corinthians 1:30,31).

Jesus Christ has become to the Christian:

Wisdom from God—the fulfillment of the salvation wrapped up in the message preached which seems so foolish to the world.

Righteousness—the One in, through, and by whom we are accepted in God's sight. Made to be "in the right" and restored to the Father's love.

Sanctification—through our relationship to Christ Jesus, we have been set apart unto God to live for His glory and His honor.

Redemption—through the shedding of Jesus' blood, the purchase of God's possession—His child, His children—has been made.

Where then is there room for men and women to boast? Before any of these things can ever be true for a man or woman or young person, he must surrender his own "wisdom" to the wisdom of God— his own authority to the authority of the Father.

Dealing with Rebels

My first day as a high school teacher brought a rude awakening. Some of my students were real rebels. I immediately began to sympathize with those educational stalwarts who for many years had valiantly stood against the onslaught of similar challenges (including myself and my friends). Now it was my turn. Friday I was a primary school teacher. Monday morning brought me face to face with the high schooler—a mysterious creature to a primary school teacher. The two environments were worlds apart.

Alex sat himself down in the very front row to my left. Sharon took herself to the chair diagonally opposite his, in the back corner of the room. All the other students filled in the gaps.

The "fun" was about to begin, and would continue for many weeks.

His hair was long, oily, and unkempt. I seem to recall a missing tooth in the "line-up" when he smiled. At any rate, Alex was the boss (of his peers). Sharon was his second-in-command. They each stood head and shoulders above the rest in physical size, myself included, and had obviously dominated the class for the whole of its time together. He sat back on the chair, letting it balance on two legs, while he plonked his feet up on the desk. Folding his arms behind his head, he allowed a sly-looking smirk to cross his lips and sat, waiting for the response this new teacher might make.

Following his lead, the whole class waited with bated breath, anxious to see if the newcomer would challenge the most dreaded student in this school of nearly eighteen hundred pupils.

Prayer took on a new dimension in the face of this battle of wits. The calm God gave to my heart sustained me in the knowledge that, while it appeared that I stood alone on the opposite side of the desk, I was fortified with the forces of my heavenly Father—against whom no man or youth or classroom could ever hope to stand.

"Take your feet off the desk and sit properly, please," I said crisply.

"Why should I?" he snapped.

"Because I am the teacher here, and you will obey me," I said without raising my voice.

He looked around at the class. A snigger arose from the group as he chirped, "Did you hear what he said? I have to *obey* him."

The calm in my voice belied the trembling within as I

waited for his obedience before doing anything further with the class. After repeated commands, and after matching retorts, Alex realized that I meant business. He threw his feet down from the desk, stood to his full height, tossed his chair under the desk, and stomped off to the new sitting position I assigned him, cursing all the way.

This episode repeated itself day after day for many weeks. I would enter that room strengthened only by the knowledge that my heavenly Father knew what was going on and that His strength was not limited in my time of weakness.

One afternoon, after enduring a similar incident, I instructed Alex to stay behind after school. I wanted to speak with him and to assign him an appropriate task as punishment for his behavior. He refused to stay and walked off angrily. I waited. Five minutes went by, then ten. As I was about to pack up my things and leave for the staff room, Alex appeared at the door. I asked him to come in, which he did. He sat down and looked at me. Our eyes locked for several moments.

"Alex, why did you come back?" I asked.

"I don't know," he replied sheepishly.

But I did. It was a surrender. A submission—and the starting point of a much friendlier relationship.

When a man's rebellious spirit toward God is melted by the power of the gospel, he returns to the authority of the Father in submission. He surrenders his position to God's position as Lord. So very foolish in the eyes of the world . . . but a picture of wisdom—God's wisdom.

> Immortal, invisible, God only wise,
> In light inaccessible, hid from our eyes,
> Most blessed, most glorious, the Ancient of Days,
> Almighty, victorious, Thy great name we praise.

That is our heavenly Father. A portrait revealing *wisdom* and *purpose*, with you and me in the center, by His grace. Let us go forth to *worship* him with our lives.

1. J. I. Packer, *Knowing God* (Downers Grove: InterVarsity Press, 1973), p. 81.

2. Ibid., p. 83.

3. Ibid., p. 81.

4. J. D. Douglas, ed., *The New Bible Dictionary* (Grand Rapids: Wm. B. Eerdmans Publishing Co., 1962), p. 1003.

5. Charles Hodge, *An Exposition of the First Epistle to the Corinthians* (London: James Nisbet and Co., 1857), p. 25.

6. T.C. Edwards, *A Commentary of the First Epistle to the Corinthians* (New York: A. C. Armstrong & Son, 1886), p. 31.

Please Don't Be Deceived

"A man either turns to God
in repentance and faith, or he runs . . . little
realizing that the only way to flee from God is to
flee to Him."

CHAPTER

3

THE DYNAMIC
OF LOVE

Did you ever try to explain something about which you knew very little? Like setting your five-year-old on your lap and proceeding to describe the intricacies of the digestive system in answer to his question, "But why don't we eat candy for breakfast?" Or try to explain what happened when your spouse finally arrived home to discover your car wrecked, piled in front of the house?

A Canadian newspaper printed a list of true statements taken from insurance forms. Here are some of the explanations, given by drivers in the heat of the moment:

> I pulled away from the side of the road, glanced at my mother-in-law and headed over the embankment.
> I had been driving for forty years when I fell asleep at the wheel and had the accident.
> The other car collided with mine without giving warning of its intention.
> I was thrown from my car as it lost the road. It was found in a ditch by some cows.

How about describing a game, the likes of which you have never seen before—ever try to do that? What were your first impressions?

My family's first encounter with American baseball was in the summer of 1983. Having purchased our tickets and the customary bucket of popcorn, we found our seats and occupied them. We watched the pregame warmups and excitedly awaited the confrontation between these two teams—Portland's Beavers against a Los Angeles team.

Having grown up with soccer, rugby-league, Australian-rules football, and cricket, baseball was going to be very different for us. New rules, difficult sayings, strange commands, unusual uniforms—and if that wasn't enough, an organ to serenade the crowd and to interpret quality of play! Later, I attempted to explain the game:

There was a man in the middle of the field, dressed in pajamas and holding a white ball. He seemed to have trouble keeping his left leg on the ground. Each time he raised his hands above his head, his leg would spring up, and he would double over in pain. He became so agitated that he threw the ball in frustration at another fellow in pajamas who kept trying to defend himself with a piece of wood. Whenever the first chap got rid of the ball, his leg problem stopped. The man with the wood got so angry at being "shot at" with the white ball that he belted it right over the fence. Obviously, the crowd was on his side because they enthusiastically applauded his aggression.

Well, the man in the middle finally ran out of frustration and stopped throwing the ball. An older man with gray hair who had been standing over to one side walked into the center to counsel the troubled chap. I think the gray-haired gentleman must have been an elder or a counselor, because after they had talked a little, the man with the ball felt very guilty and ashamed of himself and slowly walked off the field with his head hung low. They tried to cheer him up by playing the organ, but it was such a morbid song that it would have made him feel worse, I'm almost certain. He went behind a wired-in window and sat down on a bench with a row of others who, incidentally, were all dressed the same way. Perhaps they all had a similar problem with a leg or an arm. Maybe the pajamas were on too tight. Actually, it was fun watching. But they didn't seem able to "get their act together" all night because they were still running in circles when we left.

Explaining the Father

If we had to rely solely upon our own observations of God and our own interpretations of His actions in order to understand and explain God's character, we would arrive at very flawed and inadequate conclusions. We would make as big a mess of describing our heavenly Father as the man trying to explain baseball when the game is foreign to him. In the case of baseball, it does not really matter much. There is nothing of eternal significance at stake. But accuracy is of premium importance in describing our heavenly Father. For that reason, God has not left us without an accurate commentary on Himself—a truthful description of who He is, what He is like and what His purposes are for man.

The description He has left us is contained in the Bible, openly presented for all so that we may see the Person of the Lord Jesus Christ, God's Son, who affirmed, "Anyone who has seen me has seen the Father" (John 14:9b).

In Jesus Christ, God the Father is made known in truth, not in abstract, oblique terms. Many of these truths about the Father are difficult to bear. We would rather not hear them. We shy away from descriptive words like *righteous*, *holy*, and *wrathful*, because they conjure up a picture of God which is wholly different from the mental image we have formulated for our own comfort's sake.

Afraid to allow for the possibility of a God who may strongly oppose sin, we may desire to represent our heavenly Father as an all-forgiving, winking deity, who closes one eye at our sins. If that does not work, we may downplay sin to make it appear acceptable—little realizing that a thorough study of the righteousness of God will lead us to appreciate His mercy.

Men and women formulate a god of their own imaginations with whom they can feel safe and contented. They are not afraid of a god of their own making. But they *are* afraid of the God of the gospel, a God whose holiness obliges Him to challenge sin wherever it appears. It is unsettling to come face to face with such a God!

For the one who hungers to know God, for the person who longs that God be more than a stuffy collection of dry dogma—it is essential to begin by examining what the Scriptures teach regarding the character of the One whom we call *Abba*, Father.

Isaiah had a vision of the holiness of God (Isaiah 6:1-5). What did he see? It could not have been the physical stature or shape of God which overawed the prophet. We know that God is a Spirit and that those who worship Him must do so in Spirit and in truth (John 4:24). What he saw was clear. He knew what he was gazing at! He knew what he saw!

He was struck by an overwhelming awareness of the holiness, the purity, the righteousness of the living God . . . things which he could not pick up and handle . . . abstract qualities. Yet qualities obvious to a man caught in the middle of such a vision. Conscious of the holiness of God and of the utter loathsomeness of sin, Isaiah immediately cried out, "Woe is me, for I am ruined!" (Isaiah 6:5 NASB). This was no light statement. It was an interjection of deep sorrow—"*Woe is me!*"

He was in the presence of a holy God—the Almighty God whose majesty is infinite. God's holiness penetrated the life and character of Isaiah, rendering him naked before God and revealing the deep sinfulness of the creature against Yahweh's purity.

The prophet saw himself like an inkspot on the bodice of a white bridal gown. He was overcome by the awesomeness of confronting God's moral purity, by the breathtaking realization of God's holiness. He sensed the wretchedness which the writer to the Hebrews wrote about: "It is a dreadful thing to fall into the hands of the living God" (Hebrews 10:31). He could do nothing but bow in trembling recognition of his true condition before God: "Woe is me! My mouth is impure in its speech and those around me are equally foul-mouthed."

Did you ever think of Isaiah as a man of unclean lips—as being foul-mouthed? Against the prophet we may look like an inkspot. His awareness of sin is so acute, so sharp, that he refers to himself as defiled, impure.

I often think of a very dear saint whose Christlike sweetness and grace lingered in the lives of those she ministered to. This white-haired lady—of whom it would have been difficult to imagine a negative trait—once told me before we prayed together, "The older I get, the more conscious I become of sin in my life."

That is what God the Father does with His children. That is a sign of the working of God in the life of His child. The Father moves His children in the direction of holiness, toward Christlikeness, promoting in us by His Holy Spirit a consciousness of our sin and of God's moral majesty. Moses was conscious of this. "Who among the gods is like you, O LORD? Who is like you—majestic in holiness, awesome in glory, working wonders?" (Exodus 15:11).

Confronted with this crowning glory of God, Isaiah could only cry out, "Woe is me!" Later, Yahweh would speak through the mouth of this same humbled prophet, declaring His character as the only true and holy God: " 'To whom will you compare me? Or who is my equal?' says the Holy One" (Isaiah 40:25).

The Holiness of Love

An article appearing in a London newspaper recorded the views of children regarding God. Answering the questions, "Who is God?" and "What is He like?" one child said, "He is an old man and is much bigger than our house." Another replied, "He has a long white beard and wears glasses." Yet another explained, "He eats loaves and fishes for breakfast and when He takes a shower, it rains all over the place!" Amusing? Perhaps. But these childish statements no doubt mirror the notions many adults have of God.

If you were asked to paint a verbal picture of God your heavenly Father, which words would you use and which ones would you avoid? Would you major on the side of His goodness and minor on the side of His sternness? Or would you try to bring each into balance with the other? Would the portrait you paint appear in monotone, all shades of one color, or would there be contrast? Would you employ words like *kind, gracious, caring, gentle, benevolent*, exclusively? Or would you intersperse them with words like *strict, severe, disciplinarian, authoritarian*? Perhaps you would mix the colors in an attempt to make the picture more presentable, more acceptable?

It may be that life has tended to convince you of God's grace, and someone else of His mercy; while a third person may find it difficult to see anything but severity when he thinks of God. Is there no way to be certain? Is there no way to be clear on the character of our heavenly Father? Is there nothing definite that can be said?

Yes, thank God, there is! But we need to be prepared to open the Scriptures, to examine them fairly and squarely. Experiences of life will afford us illustrations of the ways God has displayed Himself to us. But the Scriptures will remain the final, underlying textbook by which to learn the right descriptive words. The Scriptures will remain the only appropriate palette from which to choose the colors we will employ in painting a portrait of our heavenly Father.

There will be some things about God we will discover we would rather not hear. There will be some words we will most probably not want to use. But we must. If we do not, our picture will be inadequate, incomplete, distorted.

It is in this area that we can become too cautious for fear that our God will be misunderstood and appear unattractive. But since He is the One who first painted His portrait for us, we must simply follow His brush strokes in the picture we paint.

C. H. Spurgeon said that it is possible for us to present the truth concerning God like a donkey chews a thistle— very cautiously!

Substitute biblical accuracy and graciousness for caution, and we are on our way. Then we will not avoid words like *righteous*, *holy* and *wrath* in reference to God our Father. But we will use them with understanding. Like the accomplished artist, we will not be afraid of the various colors. We will appreciate how they beautifully blend together to form a magnificent portrait of the most majestic Person inside or outside of the whole universe—the Christian's heavenly Father.

Clarity Is Important

' Abstract Expressionism was popularized by artists like Jackson Pollock (whose *Blue Poles* was purchased by the Australian government in the 70s for $1.5 million dollars). Pollock suspended tin cans with holes in the bottom from a wire stretched between two tripods. He laid out a canvas on the floor beneath the cans and then filled each of the cans with paint. He then set the cans in motion and allowed the paint to dribble onto the canvas below, forming its own individualized, uncontrolled pattern. Finally he selected the most satisfying area of the painted canvas to be framed and hung for display.

For those who like to "see something" in a painting, Abstract Expressionism spells frustration. Colors are just thrown together, sometimes quite literally.

The portrait Scripture paints of our heavenly Father is quite different. His characteristics are clearly distinguished. What Isaiah sensed was the dynamic of God's love, the activity, the aggressiveness, the feeling of His love in reference to sin. Isaiah referred to the holiness of love.

These two words—*holiness* and *love*—come together in a linguistic marriage to combine all other descriptions of God. Our God can be described as "Holy Love." His love is holy and His holiness is loving. The holy love of God our Father senses injury, demands justice, and expresses wrath.

Love's Sense of Injury

When God created the world, He said, "It is good" (Genesis 1:31). "I have created you out of my love," He was saying. "I have created you and I love you." "I have created you to love me." "We will live in harmony." "We will relate to each other." "We will know one another." "We will enjoy serenity and peace in this relationship of love."

The relationship God intended with His child can be likened to the cool, fresh, pure, limpid waters of a mountain stream, glistening in the sunlight: beautiful, inviting, glorious. But sin spoiled the relationship. Man rebelled, turned his back on God. The children ignored the Father.

Like the pure water that runs down into the valley where industry and residential overcrowding pollutes it by pouring into it offal and food scraps, oil and sludge—even so sin spoiled what had been so unimaginably beautiful. The children rejected the Father. They jilted the Father, they turned away His love. And the Father is moved by a sense of injury, by a sense of hurt. Someone has called it "God's most holy hurt." That hurt is expressed in His indignation.[1]

Think of a man who spends his life providing and caring for his family. He loves each child dearly. He would give his life for them. But one day each son and daughter comes to him in turn and says, "Sir, do not think of me as your child any longer—I am leaving." The father replies, "But why, my son? Why, my daughter? Have I been a bad father?" "On the contrary, you have been a very good father," each child says. "But I am tired of being under your roof, under your authority. I will become my own authority."

How is that father going to respond? How will he feel? Because he loves his children, he will be hurt. Because he loves his children, he will be indignant, displeased. Because he loves his children, he will be rightfully angry at their rejection of him and his love.

God our heavenly Father is hurt by the rejection of men. He is displeased by their actions. He is angry—and He has every right to be, because of who He is, because of His holy love.

The experience of rejected love, of a love jilted, has inspired men to do and to write beautiful things. It was the jilted love which gave birth to the hymn, "O Love That Will Not Let Me Go," and it was rejected love which brought the cross of Calvary into historical focus.

Love's Demand for Justice

Because God is holy love, because He is who He is, His every action is just. To be just is to be in the right.

When a man is "justified" by God, he is put right in God's sight (or as they translated it into the Pidgin English of a New Guinea tribe, "God, Him say, he all right"). God is in the right, and therefore He is right to judge sin and to judge sinners as guilty.

When Herbert Carson visited Australia from Bangor in County Down, Northern Ireland, he spoke of Ireland's internal strife. One of the things he said made an impression upon me. Speaking of the terrorism rampant in his country for many years, he told how many of those brought to justice have stood in the court, yelling abuse, defiant of the judge—refusing to recognize the court.

A day is approaching when every man, woman, and young person—all created beings—will stand before the judgment seat of the Holy God . . . and there will be no yelling! There will be no defiance! There will be no refusal to recognize the court! Why? Because every mouth will be silent before Him.

Habakkuk writes, "But the LORD is in his holy temple; let all the earth be silent before him" (Habakkuk 2:20). Paul writes, "Let every mouth be closed and the whole world accountable to God . . . " (Romans 3:19). God does not judge men because they are ignorant of Him, but because they try to disregard Him and His truth. Every time these rebels against God buy themselves bigger and better houses or bigger and better cars or another trip around the world—they are attempting to postpone the inevitable, to put out of their minds the fact that they must one day face God. They try to convince themselves that this life is never going to end.

Thinking they have life, they have none. They begin to create in their minds a god with whom they can be satisfied. But God is angry at anyone who rejects the accurate picture of Himself in Scripture in favor of a make-believe deity who ignores sin.

When a man rejects God, he rejects life. When a man rejects righteousness, unrighteousness increases. When a man rejects the holiness of God, ungodliness reigns.

An incident took place when I was about eleven years old. A boy who lived next door and his friend had built themselves a cubby-house in the back yard under some pine trees. This was their secret hiding place and was hidden from view by a high fence which separated their house from an adjoining paddock.

I went to see if this boy wanted to play cricket and stumbled upon the cubby-house with the two boys in it. They were surrounded by boxes of brand-new pens, candy, and stationery, and proudly announced they had stolen it from the shops along the main street in our small town.

They lamented, however, that they had been discovered by the boy's parents and were soon to be summoned before the local policeman and the shop managers. It came as a shock to them because for days they had been happily sitting in the cubby-house, rejoicing in their success. It seemed as if all was well and that no one had noticed what they had done. But they were living in a fool's paradise—and the inevitable happened.

The boy's parents loved him enough to see that he faced up to the wrong, returned the goods, and paid for what had already been consumed. The two boys were brought to justice.

God's holy love—the love of our heavenly Father—will bring the sinner to justice. That day approaches when everyone will be summoned before the living God to give an answer before the court of heaven.

A false view of love demands that justice be bypassed. God's love demands that justice be met in order that forgiveness be experienced by the sinner, and that the relationship between God the Father and His lost child be restored.

Love's Expression of Wrath

The apostle John wrote, "Whoever does not love does not know God, because God is love" (1 John 4:8). When we say God is love, when we say God is holy love, we are not

60

saying God *has* love. We are not saying that love is one aspect of God's character. We are saying that God's very nature is love—holy love—and that every other characteristic of God issues from this essential character.

Every character trait of God is part of His love: His goodness, His righteousness, His mercy, His wrath. Nowhere in the Bible are we told that God is wrath, yet there are more references in Scripture to the anger and fury and wrath of God than there are to His love and tenderness.

God gave Nahum the prophet a startling vision of the awesomeness of His character. Listen to the description Nahum left us:

> The LORD is a jealous and avenging God; the LORD takes vengeance and is filled with wrath. The LORD takes vengeance on his foes and maintains his wrath against his enemies. The LORD is slow to anger and great in power; The LORD will not leave the guilty unpunished. His way is in the whirlwind and the storm, and clouds are the dust of his feet. He rebukes the sea and dries it up. . . . The mountains quake before him and the hills melt away. . . . Who can withstand his indignation? Who can endure his fierce anger? His wrath is poured out like fire; the rocks are shattered before him. The LORD is good, a refuge in times of trouble. He cares for those who trust in him, but with an overwhelming flood he will . . . pursue his foes into darkness (Nahum 1:2-8).

God is holy love; therefore He has grace. God is holy love; therefore He has wrath. God's wrath is one aspect of His love. God's wrath is that part of His love directed toward sin.

The wrath of God is the total expression of a love that has been rejected. That is what Paul refers to when he writes, "The wrath of God is being revealed from heaven against all the godlessness and wickedness of men who suppress the truth by their wickedness" (Romans 1:18). It burns against those who reject the Father's love, against those who live as if God did not exist.

Our heavenly Father so loves the sinner that He is personally angry with everyone, every day, who refuses to know Him (see Psalm 7:11).

Augustine said of those refusing to acknowledge and to love God, "Man carries with him continually, an awareness of the wrath of God . . . an awareness that he must one day answer to the living God." The wrath of God upon the conscience, the piercing eye of God into the depths of a person's sin and guilt, is a crushing weight that a human conscience cannot bear.

So a man either turns to God in repentance and faith, or he runs . . . little realizing that the only way to flee from God is to flee to Him. When God searches the internal recesses of my heart, I want Him to record my love for Him, not my rejection. Don't you?

The eyes of God constantly survey men's hearts—ever watching, ever examining. But His observation is never passive. Habakkuk wrote of God, "Your eyes are too pure to look on evil" (Habakkuk 1:13).

Because God is who He is, He cannot allow sin to pass before Him unchallenged. Sin is against God. Sin is antilove. God cannot look on sin with favor. For God to allow sin to go unchallenged, He would have to act in contrast with His own nature—which is holy love. What loving father in his right mind could stand by and allow his child to violate every family standard of behavior without challenging the child?

It is said of David, king of Israel, that he spoiled his son Adonijah, who acted rebelliously. We read, "And his father had never crossed him at any time by asking, 'Why have you done so?'" (1 Kings 1:6 NASB). God's holiness demands that He rectify what is wrong. If God's love is not holy, then His love is false; because there can be no love apart from holiness. False love winks at wrong. True love corrects it.

Sin is not essential to humanity; it is a disease of nature. Therefore God is bent upon destroying it. Judgment of sin is the inevitable outcome of the Father's love. The

Father's loving judgment cannot be sidestepped. The Psalmist writes, "Oh, where shall I hide from the living God? If I go into the caves, You are there; if I go into hell, You will find me there!" (see Psalm 139). Men and women run from the knowledge of God, but there is no escape because the knowledge of God is an unrelenting, eternal flame that burns in the conscience. The Psalmist expressed it when he wrote:

> O LORD, rebuke me not in Thy wrath;
>   And chasten me not in Thy burning anger.
> For Thine arrows have sunk deep into me,
> And Thy hand has pressed down on me.
> There is no soundness in my flesh because of
>   Thine indignation;
> There is no health in my bones because of my
>   sin.
> For my iniquities are gone over my head;
> As a heavy burden they weigh too much for me.
> My wounds grow foul and fester.
> Because of my folly, I am bent over and greatly
>   bowed down;
> I go mourning all day long.
> For my loins are filled with burning;
> And there is no soundness in my flesh.
> I am benumbed and badly crushed;
> I groan because of the agitation of my heart.
> Lord, all my desire is before Thee;
> And my sighing is not hidden from Thee.
> My heart throbs, my strength fails me;
> And the light of my eyes, even that has gone
>   from me.

(Psalm 38:1-10 NASB)

A year or so ago, we received news that a friend in Australia was very ill and might die. This person was an invalid and our girls felt very close to him. As far as we know, he was not a Christian and had not been responsive to the gospel.

When we broke the news to our girls (who regularly prayed for our friend), they were understandably upset. My wife, Margo, and I had put the girls to bed and were sitting in the lounge room talking when we were disturbed by the sound of a child's sobbing. Margo went to investigate and discovered one of our daughters crying into her pillow. When she asked what was wrong, the little girl said through her tears, "I am crying about Mr. Jones. He does not love God. If he dies without trusting the Lord Jesus as his Savior, he will not go to be with God in heaven. I don't want him to die yet! Not before he has become a Christian."

That came as a rebuke to me. I could not recall ever having wept at the prospect of someone facing God's wrath, at the thought of someone going to hell. Out of the mouths of babes we learn!

I realized that if we cannot speak of the judgment of God without tears in our eyes, if we cannot tell of God's wrath toward sin without compassion in our hearts, if we are not moved with love toward the person who faces the endless night of God's sentence upon sin—then we need to gaze again at the cross of our Lord Jesus Christ and learn compassion there! The cross is a picture of the Father's compassion toward the sinner, where my sin is laid bare before Him and His compassion is laid bare before me.

A study of God's wrath is not as negative as it may first appear. Do you see where it has led us? A study of His wrath leads inevitably to an understanding of His mercy and grace—that which is so beautifully expressed by the hymn writer in *Grace Greater Than Our Sins*:

> Marvelous grace of our loving Lord,
> Grace that exceeds our sin and our guilt,
> Yonder on Calvary's mount outpoured,
> There where the blood of the Lamb was spilt.
>
> Sin and despair like the sea waves cold,
> Threaten the soul with infinite loss;
> Grace that is greater, yes, grace untold,
> Points to the Refuge, the mighty Cross.

Dark is the stain that we cannot hide,
What can avail to wash it away?
Look! There is flowing a crimson tide;
Whiter than snow you may be today.

Marvelous, infinite, matchless grace,
Freely bestowed on all who believe;
You that are longing to see His face,
Will you this moment His grace receive?[2]

---

1. I am indebted to G. Bingham for this and some of the other ideas expressed in this chapter.

2. Julia H. Johnston, "Grace Greater Than Our Sins." Copyright © 1910. Renewal 1938 by Hope Publishing Company, Carol Stream, IL. All rights reserved. Used by permission.

4

THE MERCY OF LOVE

One of the Puritan writers, Thomas Hooker, lay dying. A visitor, wishing to console him in the still moments prior to death, confided, "Sir, you are going to receive the reward of your labor." Hooker, fully aware that on the other side of his last breath he would stand in heaven in the presence of God the Father, responded, "Brother, I am going to receive mercy."

This man of God knew very well that he would not be receiving his just deserts. He knew that what he deserved and what he would receive were poles apart. He remained confident in the face of death; but you see, he understood the secret which lay behind his confidence. His confidence was in God. His final poise and certainty rested in the knowledge that salvation is a provision of mercy, not justice. If God were to act justly toward a sinner—in the way which is His right as the Holy God who made the universe and everyone in it—then this particular sinner's heart would fail for fear. Why? Because I would face personally the sort of justice the Father demonstrated at the cross of Calvary.

While God our Father is not obliged to stop justice from taking its course; while it is true that we each stand before God in the dock, guilty; while the inevitable course of justice need not be tampered with; nevertheless God stepped in. He took His Son—guiltless, unblemished, without sin—and subjected Him to the rigors of true justice. The Just for the unjust, the Sinless for the sinner.

But was that fair? Was that not unjust in and of itself?

Did God underreact by choosing not to punish sinful men, and overreact by punishing His own guiltless Son? Was God's notion imbalanced?

The apostle Paul anticipated the question in his letter to the church in Rome. After referring to God's choice of Jacob over Esau, he asks his readers, "What then shall we say? Is God unjust?" (Romans 9:14a) Notice the answer he gives to the question and the way he qualifies it: "Not at all!"—No, not ever! Perish the thought!—"For He says to Moses, 'I will have mercy on whom I have mercy, and I will have compassion on whom I have compassion.' It does not, therefore, depend on man's desire or effort, but on God's mercy" (Romans 9:14b-16).

Mercy, then, is the operative word. Hooker's dying statement was confident, but not self-confident. It was a statement based upon his unfaltering confidence in the mercy of his heavenly Father.

A Question to Think About

Here is a question which could be the catalyst in changing your whole life: Why should God love you?

How are you going to answer? You might say, "Well, God should love me. I became a Christian." Or "Well, you see, I'm not as bad as other people." Or "I'm a regular church-goer." Or "I've been baptized. I am a member of the church." Each of these answers (and there could be many others) implies that God is under some kind of *obligation*. But this sort of answer reveals at least two misapprehensions. First, a person answering in this way has not understood the gospel. Second, that person has not appreciated his or her true position before God.

God loved Israel as a nation and as people, and He set His affection upon her. He gave her the promised Canaan. Why did He do that? Was it because of some obvious overture of love and allegiance that Israel had pledged to God? Was it the faithfulness of this people?

Was it because of their strength as a nation? Did they have something to offer God? Was He weak without them, defeated at the thought of not having them on His side? No. Certainly not! God's own words convince us of that. He told them, "Understand, then, that it is not because of your righteousness that the LORD your God is giving you this good land to possess, for you are a stiff-necked people" (Deuteronomy 9:6). God had already made it clear that, "The LORD did not set his affection on you and choose you because you were more numerous than other peoples, for you were the fewest of all peoples" (Deuteronomy 7:7). Where does the answer lie?

An Object of the Father's Love

In Ezekiel 16:1-14 we are given an insight into God's attitude towards Jerusalem, which helps us to appreciate His mercy. Here we have a prime example of what constitutes love—an explanation of mercy:

> The word of the LORD came to me: "Son of man, confront Jerusalem with her detestable practices and say, 'This is what the Sovereign LORD says to Jerusalem: Your ancestry and birth were in the land of the Canaanites; your father was an Amorite and your mother a Hittite. On the day you were born your cord was not cut, nor were you washed with water to make you clean, nor were you rubbed with salt or wrapped in cloth. No one looked on you with pity or had compassion enough to do any of these things for you. Rather, you were thrown out into the open field, for on the day you were born you were despised.
>
> "'Then I passed by and saw you kicking about in your blood, and as you lay there in your blood I said to you, "Live!" I made you grow like a plant of the field. You grew up and developed and became the most beautiful of jewels. Your breasts were formed and your hair grew, you who were naked and bare.
>
> "'Later I passed by, and when I looked at you and saw that you were old enough for love, I spread the corner of my garment over you and covered your nakedness. I gave you my solemn

oath and entered into a covenant with you, declares the Sovereign LORD, and you became mine.

"'I bathed you with water and washed the blood from you and put ointments on you. I clothed you with an embroidered dress and put leather sandals on you. I dressed you in fine linen and covered you with costly garments. I adorned you with jewelry: I put bracelets on your arms and a necklace around your neck, and I put a ring on your nose, earrings on your ears and a beautiful crown on your head. So you were adorned with gold and silver; your clothes were of fine linen and costly fabric and embroidered cloth. Your food was fine flour, honey and olive oil. You became very beautiful and rose to be a queen. And your fame spread among the nations on account of your beauty, because the splendor I had given you made your beauty perfect, declares the Sovereign LORD.'"

One very important factor in this symbolic picture emerges. Yahweh took up the outcast child and made it the object of His love. The child was outcast, dirty, hated, squirming, and altogether unattractive. Yet God made the child the object of His love. He took this unlovely creature and embraced it with His love. Why? Because He chose to love it. As God He had the right to love, regardless of the child's appearance. He exercised His prerogative as God. That prerogative involved mercy. God's prerogative always does. The righteous Father moves in the direction of unrighteous men and women, girls and boys, displaying mercy where it is least deserved.

Created to Be Sons of the Father

God created us to be His children—men and women to be His sons and daughters. As Paul expressed it, we are to be "the image and glory of God" (1 Corinthians 11:7), reflectors of God's glory, to glorify God and to enjoy Him forever.

Mirrors are interesting. They reveal facts about the ones standing before them. They keep no secrets from the one who looks, provided he keeps his eyes open and his prejudices closed. What do you see when you look into a mirror? Is it you? Do you actually see yourself smiling back? Is that you pulling faces and waving madly?

A television advertisement designed to sell you on the quality of its color picture shows a monkey reaching out for a large, yellow banana displayed on the screen. But it is not a banana on the screen. Neither is it you in the mirror. It is an image that you see. Your image, and everything that the image does, is a reflection of you—the way it behaves itself, the way it presents itself . . . its every action and demeanor reflects you.

God's ultimate purpose in creating was to have children who reflect the glory of their Father, whose actions indicate their divine pedigree and whose behavior illustrates their divine heritage. If men and women are made in God's image, then the only way in which they will reflect God's glory is when they obey their Father's will, just as Jesus did. In other words, the Father's glory is revealed in and through the obedience of His children.

Sadly, God's children were not obedient. They were disobedient, their actions exposing them as fools (see Romans 1:22).

The only security anyone really has is the security of our Father's mercy, a mercy displayed in His Son. The writer to the Hebrews put it:

> Since the children have flesh and blood, he too shared in their humanity so that by his death he might destroy him who holds the power of death—that is, the devil— and free those who all their lives were held in slavery by their fear of death (Hebrews 2:14,15).

There is no other security. There is no other place of freedom. There is no other place of safety apart from the Father's mercy and love—the Father's embrace.

God Alone Gives Comfort

Rejecting the knowledge of God leads directly to idolatry. Relating to things in the world without reference to God, drawing comfort in life from any thing or person or attainment or achievement in isolation from God the Father, sets your feet upon the pathway which leads directly to idolatry. John described it in the incident where Jesus threw the moneychangers out of the temple:

> So he made a whip out of cords, and drove all from the temple area both sheep and cattle; he scattered the coins of the money changers and overturned their tables. To those who sold doves he said, "Get these out of here! How dare you turn my Father's house into a market!" (John 2: 15,16).

When idolatry prevails, a man's thoughts exclude the Father. Paul calls it being "futile in the mind" (Romans 1:21). It shows that a man has fallen from the glory God intended him to possess as a child of the Father. He is unable to give God glory or to reflect His glory.

In forfeiting his glory as a son, man denies God His glory as Father—as Lord. Idolatry is proof that man has exchanged the incorruptible glory of God for corruptible things—things which John called the "cravings of sinful man, the lust of his eyes and the boasting of what he has and does" (1 John 2:16).

Idolatry is a picture of foolishness that lays hands or eyes or affection upon something in the creation as a substitute for God:

Giving godly status to an object.
Granting allegiance to materialism.
Gazing with contentment upon my own achievements.
Glorying in the world.

That behavior is absurd for men and women who have been made in the image of God to commune with Him, to love and serve and adore Him, to enjoy Him forever. It is preposterous. Ludicrous. The fact is, there exists no replacement—anywhere, anytime—for the Father.

The Psalmist speaks of this same absurdity when he says of Israel: "They exchanged their Glory"—God was Israel's glory— "for the image of an ox that munches grass" (Psalm 106:20).

The prophet Jeremiah recorded Yahweh's attitude to the same absurdity: "Has a nation ever changed its gods? (Yet they are not gods at all.) But my people have exchanged their Glory"— Yahweh—"for worthless idols" (Jeremiah 2:11). Idolatry does not benefit men whatever.

This absurdity—exchanging an idol for God's glory—was most powerfully illustrated at the feet of Mount Sinai when Moses delayed from coming down the mountain. The people grew impatient and constructed for themselves a golden calf, proclaiming that it was this lump of metal that brought them out of Egypt.

When Moses finally did return, he lost his temper. The people had forsaken God to turn after a lie, an absurdity. There, before Moses' eyes, stood the crude product of men's pathetic attempt to convey the character of the true and living God in an image made of gold! He was moved with the same kind of indignation that stirred Jesus to overthrow the trading tables in the temple. He lifted the stone tablets above his head and flung them to the ground, shattering them before the people. Israel had corrupted the relationship which God revealed to Moses on the mountain (see Exodus 32).

What mother would take a photograph of the child who sat at her side and proceed to cuddle the colored piece of celluloid?

What husband would pick up a photograph of his wife who sat alongside him and proceed to hold a conversation with the Kodak image?

That is the absurdity of idolatry: seeking comfort and solace in substitutes for God, in replacements for the Father.

By convincing men and women to exchange the glory of the incorruptible God for corruptible things—ambition, houses, cars, fame, success—the Father of lies, Satan, convinces them to worship the creature rather than the

Creator. He persuades men and women to ascribe comforting qualities to the idol, to attribute fatherhood to the idol instead of to God.

The name *Father*, *Abba*, can never belong to an idol. It rightfully belongs to only One: God Himself. Only He can father you. A thing, an object, an idol, cannot. No single thing in the whole of the universe, past, present, or future, can ever father you. God is the only One who can.

The Father's Mercy in Balance

When God reveals His Fatherhood, He reveals His mercy. Yet He will not leave the guilty unpunished. To reject God's attention is to reject God Himself. To scorn God's love is to jilt the Father.

Listening to an Indian Christian speak on one occasion, I was impressed by how this ex-worshiper of the Islamic faith spoke of God as her Father. For the Muslim to speak of God as Father is to demote Him from His throne and bring Him too close to man's level. For the Islamic worshiper, calling God *Abba* is taboo—the greatest of sins. But the greatest sin a human being can actually commit is to *refuse* to recognize and glorify God as Father, as *Abba*. To jilt the Father's love is to incur the Father's judgment.

Yahweh told Moses during His unprecedented self-disclosure to Israel's leader "The LORD, the LORD, the compassionate and gracious God, slow to anger, abounding in love and faithfulness, maintaining love to thousands, and forgiving wickedness, rebellion and sin. Yet he does not leave the guilty unpunished; he punishes the children and their children for the sin of the fathers to the third and fourth generation (Exodus 34:6,7).

God withdraws His love from those who spurn it. In speaking of Israel's rejection of God's love and law, Paul the apostle points his readers to the twin characteristics of God's kindness and severity (Romans 11:22). Packer explains Paul's point by showing that "the principle which Paul is applying here is that behind every display of divine goodness stands a threat of severity in judgment if that goodness is scorned."[1]

If the Christian is chosen to the praise of God's glory, then the sinner will suffer punishment to the praise of God's justice (see Romans 9:17-23).

To accept His love, to take hold of the forgiveness which God offers you in Christ Jesus His Son, is to experience His mercy. And it is mercy a man experiences; because as a sinner, as a lost son, he has rejected the Father and should rightfully be punished.

In Jeremiah's words we see a picture of what the rejection meant for Israel as well as for the Father:

> I myself said,
> "'How gladly would I treat you like sons
>   and give you a desirable land,
>   the most beautiful inheritance of any nation.'
> I thought you would call me 'Father'
>   and not turn away from following me.
> But like a woman unfaithful to her husband,
>   so you have been unfaithful to me, O house of
>   Israel,"
>   declares the LORD.
> A cry is heard on the barren heights,
>   the weeping and pleading of the people of Is-
> rael,
> because they have perverted their ways
>   and have forgotten the LORD their God.
> "Return, faithless people;
>   I will cure you of backsliding" (Jeremiah 3:19-
> 22a).

The Lord Jesus told a parable which closely parallels the tale of Israel's rebellion. It is the story of the prodigal son, whose frustration in life convinced him he needed freedom (Luke 15:11-32). He wanted to jump out of his imagined strait-jacket, to be free. He wanted to be or do something which he thought he could never do at home where he was "so hemmed in." He was no longer satisfied to be a son. No longer interested in the home. No longer content to be a member of the family. None of these fitted in with what he wanted to be. So he left. He went away to become what he aspired to be—free. Free to be what he wanted to be. But his "freedom" led to anguish, to loneliness. He was lost. Deserted. Hungry. Alone with the pigs. He wanted to be home again, but was swamped by his unworthiness to be taken in by father and family. Smail takes it up for us:

> It was perhaps with that minimal expectation of what he could look for from his father that the prodigal came home with his modest proposal, "Make me as one of your hired servants." What wildernesses of gloomy religion lurk behind that! I can never expect to be in your dining room, drawing room, bedroom, family circle again. Give me a little lean-to behind the cowshed—I will do every duty you prescribe and otherwise keep quiet and not draw attention to myself, provided you will just put up with me! There are some very orthodox Christians who know all about the cost of the atonement who have an attitude and expectation towards God not much better or bigger than that.[2]

The love of the prodigal's father overwhelmed him. His love swept the son up in an embrace which revealed the depth of his love for his son.

The mercy, love, and kindness of God the Father can be enveloped in one word—*gracious*. In His grace, the Father bestows unmerited love upon rebellious children—and it is all with a purpose. The Lord Jesus was sent by our gracious heavenly Father in order that through His life, sacrificial death, and resurrection, lost sons and daughters might be found and restored to the Father, to the family, and to the household of God. It was the Father's intention that in being given access to the Father's love, we might live as restored sons and daughters in obedience to His standards out of gratitude for His limitless love and forgiveness.

The Father stepped in. He exercised His mercy. Paul put it, "But because of his great love for us, God, who is rich in mercy, made us alive with Christ even when we were dead in transgressions . . . " (Ephesians 2:4,5). The writer to the Hebrews says:

> For this reason he [Christ] had to be made like his brothers in every way, in order that he might become a merciful and faithful high priest in service to God, and that he might make atonement for the sins of the people (Hebrews 2:17).

The Psalmist reiterates this mercy when he writes:

> The LORD is compassionate and gracious,
>   slow to anger, abounding in love.
> He will not always accuse,
>   nor will he harbor his anger forever;
> he does not treat us as our sins deserve
>   or repay us according to our iniquities.
> For as high as the heavens are above the earth,
>   so great is his love for those who fear him;
> as far as the east is from the west,
>   so far has he removed our transgressions
>   from us.
> As a father has compassion on his children,
>   so the LORD has compassion on those who
> fear him;
>
> (Psalm 103:8-13)

Such is the love of the Father for His children. The foolish man has rejected all that. The Father offers it to you. Why?

Because as Thomas Watson, one of the Puritan writers, once commented: "The Name Jehovah carries majesty in it. The Name Father carries mercy in it."

1. J. I. Packer, *Knowing God* (Downers Grove, Ill.: InterVarsity Press, 1973) p. 148.

2. Thomas A. Smail, *The Forgotten Father* (Grand Rapids: William B. Eerdmans Publishing Co., 1980), p. 127.

CHAPTER
5

THE AGONY
OF LOVE

Parenting can be an agonizing assignment. Only a parent really understands there is something altogether unique about the relationship between a father and son or a mother and daughter. Siblings cannot share it. A single person cannot know it.

News came that there had been an accident. A gun went off. It should not have been loaded. But it was. Too late now for questions as to how and why. Fourteen is so young to die—"Will *he*?" "The doctors cannot tell yet." A bullet lodged in the boy's neck, fractions of a millimeter from vital nerves leading to the brain. *Blind*? *Deaf*? *Both*? Who knows. Only time will answer the nagging questions.

I sat outside the intensive care unit with the boy's father and grandmother. His mother had long left the scene—when the boy was a baby. "Gran" had become "Mom." We sat and waited. The painful silences were interrupted by the opening sweep of the swinging doors which ushered a nurse or doctor into the IC unit or out again. Each time, six pairs of eyes darted toward the doorway in hope of news from the surgeon, then slowly took up residence once more in the direction of the floor . . . staring but not really seeing anything. "It may take hours." And it did.

He lived. But the bullet is a permanent fixture. He must live with the uncertainty that it may dislodge at any time. Too risky to cut. So the immediate anxiety is removed . . . with a promise of more to come.

The telephone rang. A mother's voice said, "My little son liked you and the Sunday school people. Would you be happy to conduct his funeral for us?" Seven years old. A quick trip to the corner shop, but he never made it home. Never saw the car that hit him. Killed instantly. His parents proudly talked of his character traits as we sat together encircled by their family and a few close friends. They had loved him so much. Now he was gone. A cherished memory. Only the aching void remained.

Parents in pain. The agonies of love are so excruciating. We can bear only so much for ourselves, and so much less in reference to our children. To watch a son or daughter suffer defies qualification. It is agony. To watch that child die is the ultimate in torment. An accident in which the child survives brings one pain; a fatality, quite another.

But our heavenly Father intentionally endured the agony of love. Not only would He watch as His only Son suffered the agony of His earthly ministry, He agonized in giving His Son to die—in your place and mine. The Father agonized as He watched the Lord Jesus become the "man of sorrows, and acquainted with grief" (Isaiah 53:3 NASB). The Father's agony involved the Son. By looking at the pain endured by the Son, we come to appreciate something of the agony of love suffered by the Father as He looked on.

Agony in the Garden

The raising of Lazarus launched the Lord Jesus into a series of events designed by His enemies to destroy Him (Matthew 26:36- 46). But having set His face toward Jerusalem, Jesus knew the cross was in sight. Having eaten with the disciples, He went with eleven disciples to the Garden of Gethsemane. Only Judas was missing. There, eight of the disciples stayed near the entrance to the garden. The remaining three—Peter, James, and John—were taken into the quietness of the garden's center, where Jesus would pray. Here, the Son would agonize before the Father. Here, the Father would agonize before the Son.

The Agony of Isolation

Do you recall another time of isolation for Jesus? It was at the beginning of His ministry. After forty days and nights in the wilderness, the devil came and tempted Jesus—in isolation. The tempter used three enticements in trying to dissuade Jesus from the path of His pending ministry. Interestingly enough, the agony Jesus suffered in the Garden of Gethsemane at the end of His ministry was a repetition of the temptation in the wilderness—one last, violent onslaught by Satan in his attempt to prevent the inevitable obedience of the Son of God to the Father's will.

Jesus faced these two contests with the prince of darkness both times in isolation. In the first there was a triple temptation. In this final battle, Jesus prayed the triple prayer which displayed His agony: "My Father, if it is possible, may this cup be taken from me. Yet not as I will, but as you will" (Matthew 26:39b).

Jesus was isolated from men as He wrestled in the garden with the tempter. He was under the judgment of God for sinners and He wrestled with that in His humanness. With judgment over His head, our Lord knelt alone before His heavenly Father and talked with Him in prayer.

Jesus was isolated from friends in the face of the cross. Such anguish of soul and mind! The loneliest, most awesome responsibility of all time! And the disciples slept . . . He had given them opportunity to learn the truth of His suffering in His darkest hour. But they were too tired. On top of it all, our Lord experienced the hollowness of soul which Joseph had known when he was sold out by his brothers and taken down to Egypt.

The Man of men, Jesus the Man, needed His friends at this moment in a way that He had not needed them before. A friend has been defined as "one who comes in when the whole world goes out." Jesus sought companionship and support in His hour of trial. But the whole world had gone out! There were no supporters! Those who were His friends just did not understand. They fell asleep like little children who have had a long day and cannot take any more.

Jesus, the Man of men, without a friend, would show Himself as the Friend to the friendless. He would become the epitome of what the North American Indians said a true friend really is— "The one who carried my sorrows on his back."

If sympathy is two hearts tugging firmly at the one load, then Jesus stood alone from friends. Isolated to become *the* Friend of sinners. No one stood in sympathy at His side. Yet His example would inspire sympathy and courage in the hearts of others like Joseph Scriven, who, at the end of a desperate life of sorrow and isolation, would pen the words:

> What a friend we have in Jesus,
> All our sins and griefs to bear,
> What a privilege to carry,
> Everything to God in prayer.

Jesus was isolated from the Father. In His isolation He stood. He knelt. He prayed. He began to sweat drops of blood. This was no ordinary ordeal.

All the while the Father watched. He too agonized as He listened to His Son.

Jesus prayed to the Father, but He knew what was in store. The Father could not do what the Son had come to do. This was the Son's hour of isolation, and He knew it: "Now my heart is troubled, and what shall I say? 'Father, save me from this hour'? No, it was for this very reason I came to this hour" (John 12:27).

He faced the isolation of that responsibility. Jesus was alone.

Notice, however, that Jesus was not isolated from His accusers. He chose a place where He knew He could be found—the Garden of Gethsemane. He could have found a remote place; but He Himself would lay down His life. No one would take it from Him.

The Agony of Humiliation

We so often define humiliation in shallow terms. Perhaps for you, humiliation is being seen in the same dress as someone you know or having your new car bumped by a "clunker." Humiliation for our eldest daughter was once "having your father kiss you goodbye when your friends are looking." Perhaps for most of us, humiliation is being made to look foolish in front of a person whom we respect. Or perhaps humiliation, like poverty, is a state of mind induced by a neighbor's new car when you are stuck with a 1960 Chevy that loses parts each time you drive on the road.

Even our worst sense of humiliation fades into insignificance when we see what our Lord encountered. His was humiliation. Ours, hurt pride. His was real. Ours, so often imagined.

Jesus was humiliated by His disciples when they slept in the moment of His grief. The Father's unsleeping eye alone looked on. The Father's ear alone was attentive to His cry. Three times Jesus labored in prayer. Three times they slept.

Jesus was humiliated by sin. His whole being recoiled from that final and deepest humiliation in which the powers of evil inflicted upon Him the penalty of human sin— and His soul was sick with anguish.

Jesus was humiliated by anticipated death. To bow His head beneath this stroke was the last indignity. He cried, "My soul is overwhelmed with sorrow to the point of death" (Mark 14:34). That is, "My soul is sorrowful, all 'round and 'round. I am surrounded by sorrow." Here our Lord expresses the mental pain and stress that hemmed Him in on every side, from which there was no escape.

The Agony of Obedience

In Jesus, the horror of death and the zeal of obedience met. Jesus must submit Himself to the scorching furnace of divine wrath. He must suffer and die.

Here in the garden the process began. Here the second Adam would determine to obediently restore that which had been ruined by the first.

Jesus was obedient to His mission. There could be no washing away of sins without the shedding of his blood. "Take this cup from me . . . " suggests a sense of despondency and of depression; yet our Lord's heart and mind were set upon the Father's will. It was here, at the onslaught of depression, that Jesus turned to the Father in prayer.

Jesus was obedient despite the cost. He did not shrink from the responsibility. He directed His face toward

Jerusalem saying, "But I have a baptism to undergo, and how distressed I am until it is completed!" (Luke 12:50). He reached the goal of His work by rendering full obedience in the most trying circumstances. The temptation came—"remove the cup"—but He repelled it.

Jesus was obedient to the Father's will. By His suffering, our Lord learned the full weight of obedience. His determination was reflected in His rebuke of Peter:

> Peter took him aside and began to rebuke him. "Never, Lord!" he said. "This shall never happen to you!" Jesus turned and said to Peter, "Out of my sight, Satan! You are a stumbling block to me; you do not have in mind the things of God, but the things of men" (Matthew 16:22,23).

These were the beginnings of our Lord's personal sorrows. He would agonize from this point to the other side of the cross. Throughout the length of His suffering, the Father endured an agony made more acute by the knowledge that His beloved Son must endure alone.

The cup of sorrow thickened—yet our Lord drank it.

Remind yourself, "He drank it for me, as if I alone among men had need to be saved." "My soul," said Jesus, "is overwhelmed with sorrow to the point of death"—yet He faced it for me.

Remind yourself that "my sin pressed upon His soul"—

My self-centeredness
My pride
The sin of my youth
The sin of my manhood or womanhood
The sin of my heart, my lips, my thoughts

My sin pressed on His soul with the grip of a vise—and wrung from Him the cry of anguish.

> The powers of hell, united, pressed,
> And squeezed His heart and bruised His breast,
> What dreadful conflicts raged within,
> When sweat and blood forced through His skin.

Our Lord's prayer to the Father so penetrated the halls of heaven as to gain Him strength through communion with the Father. Our Champion, our great Deliverer, received strength from God and rose to face His final battle with sin. The cup was not drained until the cry of desolation sounded forth across the valley—"My God, my God, why have you forsaken me?" (Matthew 27:46).

I am saved because He was obedient. Did you realize that? Mark it well! Did you ever stop to think that if Jesus had escaped the penalty of sin, you would still be facing it? Those who continue to refuse God's grace still face it.

Abraham Lincoln left a fine legacy for historians to ponder. He once took a short journey in a horse-drawn carriage with two fellow lawyers. From the window of his carriage he noticed on the ground two little birds that had fallen from their nest in a tree. He insisted that the driver stop to let him out so that he could rescue the birds. Later, he told how he spent hours walking home to the laughter of his friends. Listen to how Lincoln explained his actions: "I could not rest until I had returned them to their mother."

Jesus' love was like that, but infinitely greater. He could not rest until He had restored lost sons of God to their Father. That took the agony of love. Both Father and Son agonized over lost sons in order to restore the family.

Are you getting the picture?

6

THE SACRIFICE OF LOVE

The day came when an enormous aircraft swallowed up our family in Sydney, Australia, and coughed us up in Los Angeles, U.S.A. After being in transit for thirty hours, suspended forty thousand feet above the earth for most of that time, we were ready for a warm welcome and a good night's sleep. Neither happened—no welcome, no sleep. Just the beginning of a fresh ordeal.

Two adults and three little girls. Back-packs full to the brim, weighing down the frame of each tired child. Both arms of each parent stretched to the limit just carrying suitcases. Five pairs of legs weary at the long trek through a labyrinth of underground walkways linking international and national terminals. One hundred and nine degrees (air conditioning out of action). Third-degree smog enveloping the city in a pollution bubble. More people in one place than we had ever encountered before, yet no one to talk to. Hot, weary, frustrated, lonely, uncertain . . . at the dropping point in a strange place.

I have never felt so abandoned. We wanted home. But where was it? Somewhere over our shoulders, approximately ten thousand miles southwest. Stranded in the midst of a different world—marooned in a sea of uncertainty. Our sense of abandonment felt real. But our heavenly Father had never left our side.

Have you ever felt abandoned?

Martin Luther felt the pain of abandonment at the Diet of Worms. His ninety-five theses, nailed to the door of the castle church in Wittenberg, became the spark which kindled an explosion in ecclesiastical strongholds. Luther had denounced the corruption permeating the established church. He sought debate . . . but reaped anger. He acted out of biblical conviction . . . but was called a heretic.

He found himself before the Diet and at the mercy of the Emperor. Accused by his ecclesiastical colleagues of being an enemy of the Church, the Augustinian monk left the Diet and began his journey home—apparently abandoned.

Yet Luther was not without friends, friends who were greatly alarmed at the prospect of his murder. Plots had already been lodged against his life, and the journey homeward promised to be perilous. As his carriage entered a narrow pass, it was suddenly surrounded by five horsemen—masked and completely armed.

Without a word, they forced Luther to alight, threw a cloak over his shoulders, placed him on an extra horse, then disappeared into the forest with their captive.

The brave monk was taken to the Castle of Wartburg which lay hidden in the mountains. There the clanging of chains was heard as the gates opened and the party of horsemen entered the courtyard. His ecclesiastical garb was removed, he was clothed in the garments of a knight and christened Knight George.

During the next ten months, Luther translated the Scriptures into the language of his people. Why? Because he was not in the hands of enemies, but protected by his friends. Frederick the Elector had taken steps to protect his friend, whom he would not abandon in his darkest hour.

Have you ever felt abandoned? Abandoned by friends? By parents? By children? By employer? Even by God?

Hagar felt its brunt at the hands of Sarah, who told Abraham, "Get rid of that slave woman and her son, for that slave woman's son will never share in the inheritance with my son Isaac" (Genesis 21:10). So Hagar was put out into the wilderness of Beersheba where she wandered about forlorn, deserted. Yet she was not alone. God heard her boy's cry and understood their plight. He cared for them. Unlike the others, God would not desert them.

Nebuchadnezzar felt abandoned by God Himself (Daniel 4:28- 37). He had become proud, interpreting his kingship as proof of his autonomy and power. He fell at the sweep of God's chastening hand—and he did not get up for seven years. He did not sit on his kingly throne again until he acknowledged God as the only true and living Sovereign, the Ruler of heaven and earth, Who alone is worthy of the praise and glory of men.

Jesus, the Man central to all of history, the One in whom God the Father would display His own grace and love from Bethlehem to Calvary to the resurrection and beyond—this Jesus, our Savior, knew what it was to be abandoned, both from the hand of men and the hand of the Father.

Abandoned to Die

In Matthew 27:37-54 it becomes painfully clear that our Lord Jesus was abandoned in His darkest hour. This man, "a man of sorrows, and acquainted with grief," was Himself abandoned to die.

Love would now demand its sacrifice. The sacrifice of love would involve the Son. Love's sacrifice would mean abandonment for the Son and heartache for the Father: Love's sacrifice would cost the Son His life and the Father His Son.

But the sacrifice would be made and love would be vindicated—proved true and authentic both in the Father and in the Son.

Abandoned by Peter and the Disciples

Peter's mind was confused, a jumble of thoughts. Jesus was different somehow.

He had rebuked Peter's swing with the sword which sliced off an ear. He greeted Judas with compassion—and here from the courtyard Peter could see Jesus, bent and weakened from the beating He had received.

He had not retaliated! There was blood on His face,

but . . . . He said nothing!

He just took it—all of it—like a lamb before the slaughter.

How Peter loved his Lord! How his heart ached for Jesus! But . . . wasn't He the King? If He kept up this approach, He could be killed! Peter and the disciples could all be killed!

As the apostle stood there, far away in thought, a servant girl burst in upon his silence: "You also were with Jesus of Galilee" (Matthew 26:69).

Fear shot through Peter's veins like an electric charge. He denied the accusation vehemently, saying, "I don't know what you're talking about" (Matthew 26:70).

Peter moved away, only to be discovered by another servant girl who also recognized him. But he denied any acquaintance with Jesus: "I don't know the man!" (Matthew 26:72).

Finally, the thing which distinguishes a New Yorker from a Southerner, an Aussie from a Yankee, gave him away. It was his accent: "Surely you are one of them, for your accent gives you away" (Matthew 26:73).

He began to curse and swear. He let forth with that final blast of denial—"I don't know the man!" Then Peter heard the rooster crow, and he melted. He remembered his bold statement to Jesus, that he of all people would never deny his Lord (Matthew 26:35).

Peter had abandoned his Friend and Lord, and he knew it.

In personal defeat, he went out of that place and wept bitterly. Peter was safe . . . but Jesus stood abandoned. Peter left . . . but Jesus was led away very much alone.

Peter's world fell on top of him. His hopes, dreams, expectations, plans—all dashed if Jesus was not who He said He was.

Peter had worked it out as it was supposed to be. The Lord's way seemed all wrong. But Peter had not yet set in order the pieces. He had not yet grasped the context in which Jesus was operating—that is, the sacrifice of love.

When Jim and Elisabeth Elliot set out to go to the Auca

Indians, they too had their hopes and dreams and expectations for ministry. Suddenly, Jim and the others were martyred. The world of Elisabeth Elliot came tumbling down.

What would you do? It would seem natural to cry out, "Lord! There has been some mistake! Lord, this is not the way we planned it! You do not appear to be in control, Lord! Everything's run amok!"

Have you ever felt that way? Ever expressed it like that? Do you remember what the Lord tried to say in the midst of your frustration? Do you recall the gentle way He came to you in your calm after the storm and whispered, "Trust Me. I know what I am doing. I have it worked out perfectly. Do not abandon Me. Have confidence in Me."

In this case, missionaries lost their lives—but God established a church among the Aucas. He was working out His purposes. Love still prevailed, even though it appeared veiled at the time.

What Peter failed to see (and what we often fail to see) is that God was doing it His way; and His way is always best. He was teaching Peter dependence upon his Lord rather than upon his own strength—of which this apostle had loudly boasted. Peter was witnessing the sacrifice of love, designed by the Father and implemented by the Son. It meant standing alone, without retaliation. It meant not opening his mouth.

Abandoned by Pilate and the Authorities

His disciples had deserted Him. The lone, silhouetted figure of our Lord now stood against the backdrop of a hateful crowd.

At their head stood the Roman governor, Pilate, whose only remembered role on the stage of history was this one. Even non-Christian historians only mention Pilate in reference to his authorizing Jesus' death. He has no other claim to fame.

Pilate allowed the people's conscience to be his own (Matthew 27:22-25). The people's will, not his own conscience, became Pilate's rule. And then from the lips of this man came one of the most ironical statements in history. He said, "I am innocent of this man's blood."

But was he?

Those in positions of authority can never be innocent in such matters. Pilate was in a position to act in favor of Jesus, but he abandoned the Man of Sorrows. He was intimidated by the rabble. He set popularity against justice, and acted against his conviction that Jesus was innocent.

While activity mounted on the grounds of Pilate's residence, another man sat quietly in his cell in the prison. His name was Barabbas, a convicted criminal. We can imagine what happened as he sat listening. He was conscious of the rabble outside. He listened again, straining for details.

The cries of the rabble grew louder. He heard the crowd's reply to Pilate's question, "Which of the two do you want me to release to you?" It sounded through the walls with increasing volume: "Barabbas! Barabbas! Barabbas!"

He heard their reply to Pilate's question, "What shall I do, then, with Jesus who is called Christ?" Now their cries sounded with shrill intensity: "Crucify, crucify him! Crucify! Crucify!"

His heart began to pound. He heard the rhythmic marching of soldiers' feet as they came closer and grew louder. They stopped outside his cell. He waited to hear what his pounding heart feared the worst. The captain of the guard spoke: "Barabbas, stand to your feet." His heart was beating now at full pace. Then he heard it.

"Barabbas. You are a free man."

"What? Me? I have been tried and found guilty. What do you mean I am a free man?"

We can imagine the captain of the guard looking this criminal right in the eye and saying, "Did you ever hear of the man Jesus? Well, He just went to die on your cross."

When Jesus was abandoned to die in place of Barabbas, He was abandoned to die in your place and in mine. That is love in action. That is the sacrifice of love.

Abandoned by the People

Mockery and scorn, scoffing and derisive laughter were not new to our precious Lord. Men had been wagging their heads at Him for a long time. Peter tells us that Christ was blasphemed in the time of Noah—since He was there in

Spirit—and was rejected by all but eight people (see 1 Peter 3:18ff.) He has been scorned for a long time.

The rulers and authorities, the rank and file . . . so many of the people despised the Son of God. They were blinded to His identity and uncomfortable by His presence. Our Lord was unpopular because His very presence as the Light sent from God revealed sin for what it is.

It was a jungle which Jesus faced that day.

There were demons in the crowd.

The people were intimidated by each other.

The nastiness of men's hearts without God was arrayed like no other day in history.

I'm reminded of an incident in San Francisco's Union Square when Christian young people were giving verbal witness at a rally to their faith in Jesus Christ as Lord and Savior. Suddenly, the park was inundated with homosexuals dressed as nuns and carrying black, helium-inflated balloons, their faces painted and their feelings ugly. Lines of them, accompanied by undecorated supporters, yelled out, blew whistles, shouted abuse, and generally attempted to destroy any witness to Christ as the Son of God and the Light of the world.

Yet on that day, the aggressors' intentions were thwarted. The response of those young Christians registered a resounding victory for the Name of Christ. Without fighting back, without reviling or scrapping in any way, these believers allowed the Holy Spirit to use them to the glory of Christ. They offered no reciprocal agitation; and in time, even the honest members of the "marauding band" had to confess that the genuineness of Christian love prevailed. The Christians later mingled among the crowd and boldly approached any of the offenders who had the courage to remain behind to speak with them.

Here, in the incident in Union Square, we see the state of a man's heart, a woman's heart, a child's heart, without Christ Jesus. It was the same on the day of Jesus' crucifixion. Certainly, the Father was working out His purposes. True, Satan was agitating in the crowd. It is a fact that darkness was irritated by the presence of the light. But man's heart revealed its own sin also.

A little girl was mean to her brother and he went crying to their mother. "Why have you let Satan put it into your heart to pull your brother's hair and kick his shins?" she asked. The little girl thought for a moment, then replied: "Maybe Satan did put it into my head to pull my brother's hair, but kicking his shins was my own idea."

We need to notice that when the people rejected Jesus, their hearts were in it. A great deal of a man's sin is his own idea.

Abandoned by the Father

The sacrifice of love was yet to reach its most excruciating point for both the Father and the Son.

The road of obedience is the road of suffering. Jesus took that road to the cross—an agony foretold in Psalm 22:1 and confirmed by our Lord's own words in Matthew 27:46.

Abandoned. Forsaken by the Father. How could we even begin to describe the suffering of being separated from God the Father?

I remember as a little boy being coaxed by my teacher to look up at an eclipse of the sun through a pin-hole in a piece of card. Eclipse was hard enough for me to pronounce, much less to understand. I did not have a single clue. I have since discovered that a solar eclipse is the obscuring of the sun when the moon comes between it and the earth. One comes between the other.

Now, Jesus' cry of utmost anguish—"My God, my God, why have you forsaken me?"—heralded a rupture, an eclipse, in the relationship between Father and Son. It was as if hell rolled between Jesus and the heavens, cutting off the lines of communication.

The jaws of hell yawned open, anxious to engulf the Christ. The Lord Jesus hung on a tool of primitive torture, His body palpitating with searing pain, His soul conscious of desertion by the Father.

He did not cry out, "Why did Peter abandon Me?"

He did not wail, "Why did Pilate abandon Me?"

He did not plead, "Why did the people abandon Me?"

He cried out with a loud voice, "My God, My God, why hast *Thou* abandoned Me?"

He had lost all sense of the Father's favor. He had become what John calls our "propitiation." He had become the wrath bearer—the offering through which God, who had previously shown His wrath toward the sinner, is now able to bestow His favor.

Peter was intimidated by his peers.

Pilate was intimidated by the rabble.

The people were intimidated by each other . . . and all because of Jesus.

Peter was safe from a big mistake, he thought.

Pilate won votes.

The people felt secure.

But Jesus stood alone, abandoned to die.

Personal grief wrung from him the personal cry! His whole soul ached. *He hung.* It was not the nails that kept Him there. He could have called thousands of angels to come and rescue Him. It was not the nails—it was His love that kept Him there.

Jesus was the example of true man. The Man, for men. The Father's Son, given.

This was the darkest hour in history. Darker than the night Rome was burned, beginning the Emperor Nero's awful persecution of Christians. Darker than the Crusades which brought bloodshed in the name of Christianity. Darker than the Holocaust, engineered by Hitler and his evil regime, which seemed almost to bring hell to earth and signal the end of the world. Darker than the deepest well of depression into which a man or a woman might fall.

Golgotha, the Place of the Skull, became the setting for the darkest hour in history. Here at the cross, the Lord Jesus was abandoned to the horrors of hell . . . abandoned for the sake of sinners.

At the cross, an unbearable weight pressed down upon Jesus' heart . . . and He bore it.

At the cross, the sinless Son of God took the punishment for such heinous human crimes as the persecutions and Crusades, the Holocaust, and every sin from the time of Adam's first act of rebellion to my last unkind thought.

At the cross, Jesus met sin head on. He went down into the depths of hell where a battle raged. Sin took hold of our Lord and poured out all of its vile ugliness upon Him, battering and pelting Him with demonic fury and every hideous force at its disposal—until it was totally exhausted.

Jesus emerged the victor. Sin could not prevail over the moral purity and power of the Son of God. We shout praise to His Name—King Jesus!

The King has triumphed! In His majesty He has restored what was lost in the Garden of Eden.

He is the second Adam, the life-giving Spirit (see 1 Corinthians 15:45). No wonder He could turn to the repentant thief on the cross and say, "Today you will be with me in paradise" (Luke 23:43). He made possible our restoration to the tranquility and peace of a relationship God intended from the very beginning of creation.

No wonder He could cry, "It is finished." No wonder we cry, "Who shall separate us from the love of Christ?"

Paul the apostle wrote:

> For I am convinced that neither death nor life,
> neither angels nor demons, neither the present
> nor the future, nor any powers, neither height
> nor depth, nor anything else in all creation, will
> be able to separate us from the love of God that
> is in Christ Jesus our Lord (Romans 8:38,39).

As soon as we share the love of God, we will share the sorrow of God . . . if we begin to get a glimpse into the pain endured by the Man of Sorrows in His mission to restore you and me—lost sons—to the Father. Such is the sacrifice of love.

That is what it cost the Son, and that is what it cost the Father.

Jesus was abandoned that we might not be. He was forsaken that the soothing tones of the Father's words might be directed toward us: "Accepted in the Beloved—accepted in my Son."

The Father offers you this love at this very moment. Every lost son of God who turns his back on sin and embraces by faith the work of his Substitute, Jesus, is instantly forgiven and adopted into the family of God. This gift was not cheap—but it is offered to you free.

How will you respond?

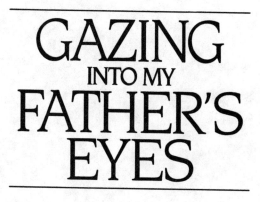

GAZING
INTO MY
FATHER'S
EYES

I'm So Glad
I Know Him

"Our God, our heavenly Father,
is both personal and within the reach
of His children. In fact, He has shown us that even
when our reach seems too short, His is always
long enough. He has never retracted His
outstretched arms from His people."

CHAPTER
7
PERSONAL, ALWAYS REACHABLE

One of the many things I loved about my father while I was growing up was that he was always available. Now, he *was* busy. What pastor is not? He just made time. It was not always at the very moment I nominated, but it was as soon as possible.

I used to love to play soccer—ate it, dreamt it, planned it, practiced it, played it. A great game! Snow, rain, cold weather, warm weather, not even nightfall seemed able to dampen my enthusiasm for the sport. But no sport, regardless of its attraction, gives maximum joy unless it is shared with someone . . . someone to watch as you make that fantastic shot at goal . . . to cheer as you execute a long run . . . to shout encouragement as you help set up the winning score.

For a young boy, the very best thing of all is to have your father as that someone. My father would run up and down the sideline, never missing an important play. A sideward glance would assure me that he had seen my "feat." At halftime he would bring out cut oranges for the players to drink for their energizing juices, readying them for the second half. He would stand and listen as the coach beat our eardrums with words of "soccer wisdom" and pat our backs as we rose to do battle again with the team from the neighboring town. My father was available. He was within reach. That set him apart from so many of the other boys' fathers who simply were never there.

There was more to this relationship, however, than my father's being within reach of his son. I knew him. And he knew me. In the crowd he would recognize me, and in a gathering of people I would recognize him. My father was not "that kind man who takes an interest in my activities." He was always "Dad." Whether in the formal setting of public gatherings or on the sideline of a soccer game, this was my dad. I knew him by experience and I knew him by title, a title exclusively his. My lips and heart would not and could not ever claim that title for any other. This one who was known by others under various titles—Mr. Law, Rev. Law, Alex Law, Pastor Law—was really none of those things to me. Our relationship was too personal to be spoiled by the formality of any of these. He could only be one thing if the relationship was to be personal: He had to be *my dad*.

The Personal Nature of a Title

Some people can be identified by their titles: "husband," "president," "chairman," "daughter," "king," "mechanic." Others are known by more casual titles we call nicknames. An Australian male with red hair will very often gain the moniker "Blue." It's not unusual to hear an Aussie greet his red-headed friend by saying, "Gidday Blue. How are ya goin', mate?"

How we use names often shows our relationship to someone. It can show that we know him *personally*. It is like that with God. We can know Him *personally*, not only through our experience of Him, but in particular through His titles.

The very titles by which we refer to God will describe everything we have experienced Him to be. But because our experiences (joy or sorrow, hardship or suffering) may prompt us to misinterpret God's character, for an accurate view we must examine the titles God places upon Himself rather than relying upon our own limited assessments of His character.

The nickname "Blue" may tell us that a man has red hair, but it does not tell us much else about the person. The titles God uses of Himself in the Bible combine to tell us everything we need to know about Him. What we discover through an examination of these titles is that God our Father, while remaining the God above all gods whose Name is to be hallowed, is both *personal* and *reachable*.

God's Self-Revelation in Titles

God is not God's name. In Hebrew the word *El* means "god" in the broadest sense. While the title connotes power, even supernatural power, it can just as easily be applied to a false god—to an object or image given god-status.[1] To simply speak of "God" is not enough. That title may apply to false gods.

While the name *God* is used more than six thousand times in Scripture, we could not come to personally appreciate God's character unless he disclosed it to us through other qualifying titles. In Exodus 3:13, Moses asks God, "What is [your] name?" The Lord replies, "I am who I am." This comes from the Hebrew verb *hayah*, which means "to be" and is rendered variously "I am," "I am what I am," and "I will be what I will to be." It is a name that tells us so much, and yet cannot easily be expressed in a simpler title than "I am." It tells us among other things that:

God is *unique*	". . . I am God, and there is no other; I am God, and there is none like me" (Isaiah 46:9).
God is *self-sufficient*	"Who has understood the Spirit of the Lord, or instructed him as his counselor? Whom did the Lord consult to enlighten him, and who taught him the right way? Who was it that taught him knowledge or showed him the path of understanding?" (Isaiah 40:13,14).
God is *unchangeable*	"I the Lord do not change. So you, O de-descendants of Jacob, are not destroyed" (Malachi 3:6).
God is *holy*	"I am the Lord your God; consecrate your-selves and be holy, because I am holy . . ." (Leviticus 11:44a)
God is *eternal*	"Do you not know? Have you not heard? The Lord is the everlasting God, the Creator of the ends of the earth. He will not grow tired or weary, and his understanding no one can fathom" (Isaiah 40:28).

Why has God not left us with a simple title by which to name Him? Because His character and personality cannot be encapsulated, hemmed into, or summed up in a single name. Instead, God has filled His Name with meaning. "I Am" has become pregnant with significance. Throughout redemptive history, God has made Himself known in increasingly personal terms: *Yahweh- jireh* (I Am-Provider, see Genesis 22:8,14); *Yahweh-nissi* (I Am- [your] Banner, see Exodus 17:15); *Yahweh-shalom* (I Am-Peace, see Judges 6.24); *Yahweh-tsidkenu* (I Am-Righteousness, see Jeremiah 23:6, 33:16); *Yahweh-shammah* (I Am—[your] Everlasting Presence, see Ezekiel 48:35—the Lord is there, ever present, ever within reach).[2]

God's Self-Revelation As Father

This same Yahweh has constantly expressed His longing for a personal relationship with His children whom He made to love, glorify, and enjoy Him forever. He has continuously revealed His affection for His sons and daughters; but their sin has stood in the way of that relationship. The prophet Jeremiah, with superlative tenderness, voices the yearning of Yahweh for the personal loyalty and love of His people:

> "Then I said,'How I would set you among My sons,
> And give you a pleasant land,
> The most beautiful inheritance of the nations!'
> And I said, 'You shall call Me, My Father,
> And not turn away from following Me.'"
> (Jeremiah 3:19 NASB).

Isaiah, noting that the people's sins had so sullied their image as God's children as to render their family status unrecognizable, noted also the consistency of the Father's faithfulness toward His people:

> Look down from heaven and see
> from your lofty throne, holy and glorious.
> Where are your zeal and your might?

Your tenderness and compassion are with-
   held from us.
But you are our Father,
   though Abraham does not know us
   or Israel acknowledge us;
you, O LORD, are our Father,
   our Redeemer from of old is your name.
      (Isaiah 63:15,16)

George Foot Moore observed the personal qualities of
God the Father in relation to His children and His gracious
devotion even in the face of their sin:

> In the rabbinical literature the paternal-filial re-
> lation between God and man is a common
> theme. R. Akiba's words have already been
> quoted ... "Beloved (of God) are the Israelites,
> in that they are called sons of God; still more be-
> loved in that it is made known to them that they
> are called sons of God" (Deut. 14:1). R. Judah
> (ben Ila'i) thought that the name sons was given
> them only when they behaved themselves like
> sons, but R. Meir refuted him by quoting pas-
> sages in which they were called foolish sons (Jer.
> 4:22), untrustworthy sons (Deut. 32.20), breed of
> evil-doers, vicious sons (Isa. 1:4)—but sons not-
> withstanding. Instead of its being said to them,
> Ye are not my people, they shall be called sons
> of the living God (Hos. 2:1). The relation is not
> annulled by sin.
>
> The fatherly care of God for Israel is a familiar
> idea in Scripture. R. Judah ben Ila'i says on
> Exodus 14:19 ("The angel of God who went be-
> fore the camp of Israel removed and went be-
> hind them"). "A rich verse the idea of which is
> found in many places." "It is like a man who was
> walking on the way and letting his son go on be-
> fore him; came robbers in front to take the boy
> captive, the father put him behind him; came a
> wolf from behind, he put him in front; came

robbers in front and wolves behind, he took him up in his arms; did he begin to be troubled by the heat of the sun, his father stretched his own garment over him; was he hungry, he gave him food, thirsty, he gave him to drink. Just so God did, as it is written," etc. He led Israel, His son, and took it in His arms (Hos. 11:1-3); spread over it a cloud to shelter it from the heat (Ps. 105:39); fed it with bread from heaven (the manna, Exod. 16:4), brought streams out of the rock for it to drink (Ps. 78:16). God has compassion as a father on His sons (Ps. 103:13) . . . [4]

God's Ultimate Self-Revelation in the Son

The Father's self-revelation reached its zenith in Jesus Christ, His Son. Jesus Himself said, "Anyone who has seen me has seen the Father" (John 14:9). This was more than saying that He very much resembled the Father. Throughout His earthly ministry, Jesus performed signs and miracles, each a demonstration pointing to the redemption He offered—signs which indicated that Jesus was more than just One Who appeared to have similar qualities as the Father. What Jesus did placed Him on a spiritual par with the Father. His miracles confirmed that His essential nature was the same as the Father's. Consequently, Jesus acted as the Son of God could be expected to act. He spoke the truth when He said, "I and the Father are one" (John 10:30). That is, a unity. United in nature, in purpose—of one essence.

John the apostle records for us the following statements of Jesus:

> I am the bread of life—John 6:35
> I am the light of the world—John 8:12
> I am the gate for the sheep—John 10:7
> I am the good shepherd—John 10:11
> I am the resurrection and the life—John 11:25
> I am the way and the truth and the life—John 14:6
> I am the true vine—John 15:1

On each of these occasions, the Son of God qualified His "I am's." But on several other occasions He did not. And the Jewish leaders, at those times, interpreted His remarks as blasphemous because He spoke so freely of the father-son relationship between Himself and God.

The high priest asked Jesus:

> "Are you the Christ, the Son of the Blessed One?" "I am," said Jesus. "And you will see the Son of Man sitting at the right hand of the Mighty One and coming on the clouds of heaven." The high priest tore his clothes. "Why do we need any more witnesses?" he asked. "You have heard the blasphemy . . . " (Mark 14:61-64a).

In the Garden of Gethsemane, on the night that Jesus was betrayed, Judas Iscariot, the Roman battalion, and officers from the chief priests and the Pharisees all confronted Jesus and the disciples. John tells us:

> Jesus, knowing all that was going to happen to him, went out and asked them, "Who is it you want?" "Jesus of Nazareth," they replied. . . . When Jesus said, "I am he," they drew back and fell to the ground (John 18:4-6).

This text does not explain why those opposing Jesus fell to the ground when He said, "I am he." But it seems reasonable that those who fell back were probably Jews, and that they were responding to what they interpreted as blasphemy. They fully expected Jesus to be struck down for making such a claim.

In John 8:58 we have recorded for us the most powerful declaration made by Jesus concerning His identity.

Answering the Pharisees, who were attempting to pit their "Abrahamic pedigree" against His authority, Jesus said: "I tell you the truth, before Abraham was born, I am!" (John 8:58).

Jesus called Himself by Yahweh's Name. He used the very same title that God had used to refer to Himself. He said, "I am the Eternal One"—and He offered no apology for the statement.

It is clear that the Jewish leaders understood Jesus' words in this way because of their violent reaction: "At this, they picked up stones to stone him . . . " (John 8:59)

The pinnacle of God's self-revelation has been reached in Jesus Christ, God's Son. Jesus stood before the world to declare the Father—a tangible, living description of the One Eternal God, brought into reach. He made known God's "Christian Name," God's Personal Name . . . the Name *Father*. To know Him as Father is to know Him as both personal and reachable.

Three stanzas of an eighteenth-century hymn express the delight and comfort this brings to a child of God:

> My God, my Father, blissful Name!
> O may I call Thee mine!
> May I with sweet assurance claim
> A portion so divine!
>
> This only can my fears control,
> And bid my sorrows fly,
> What harm can ever reach my soul
> Beneath my Father's eye?
>
> Whate'er Thy sacred will ordains,
> O give me strength to bear;
> And let me know my Father reigns,
> And trust His tender care.
>
> (Anne Steele, 1717-78)

The Personal Qualities of Father

We walked along the beach. Well bundled up against the cold, and conscious of little else besides the next reply to a question previously asked, our conversation made us oblivious to time and schedules. We simply walked on, listening one minute and responding the next. Bill had just made an interesting remark. In reference to something he had heard a preacher say, he mused, "That was liberating to me."

"What was it?" I asked, now even more interested.

"The fact that God just wants you to be a son," he replied.

110

The implications of that thought had for so long thrilled my heart that by now I was ready to walk on—and talk on, despite the cold.

"Please tell me more," I said. "How has that helped you?"

My companion, hands in pocket and face fixed in the direction of the seemingly endless beach that stretched out ahead, began to explain. Each time he spoke, a cloud of condensed air shot from his mouth, a reminder of the chill in the air.

"I had spent my whole life trying to be something that I was not, desperately trying to please," he said. "I strained for the approval and acceptance of my earthly father, but found that acceptance carried a high price tag. I battled through my childhood and teenage years, exerting every effort to be what my father wanted in a son. I wanted to please him."

His father had been severe, a dictator of life and family with very set ideas about how a boy should be reared and what interests should delight him. Over the years Bill would hear his father say, "You may not love me, but you will respect me!"

Bill continued.

"I took up boxing and football in an attempt to create the image that my father craved in his son, but it was not me. I tried to be outwardly tough, but inwardly I was just a marshmallow."

Bill turned to drugs and became addicted. Now, years later, I walked on the beach alongside a man who had made the most liberating discovery of his life—"God just wants me to be a son."

God our heavenly Father does not want us to be anything we are not. He does not delight in facade. Sham qualities bring Him no pleasure. It is His desire that His children be themselves and delight in the privileges of uniqueness without fear of rejection from the Father. He desires that His children live holy lives within a family in which there is mutual acceptance. Family members are approved and accepted on the basis of the total acceptance bestowed by the Father upon all those who have come into the family through faith in the redeeming work of the Son of God at Calvary.

Bill's earthly father seemed out of reach. Impersonal. Bill could never quite make the grade. It was so emancipating to follow Jesus across the bridge He built across the gap previously separating the Father and lost children. There, Bill made a wonderful discovery: "God just wants me to be a son."

And what was the most liberating part of that discovery? Not only did God want Bill as a son, but God Himself wanted to be a personal Father to Bill. As a personal Father, God cares for His children.

Peter the apostle told the scattered Christians to whom his letter was addressed:

> Humble yourselves, therefore, under God's mighty hand, that he may lift you up in due time. Cast all your anxiety on him because he cares for you (1 Peter 5:6,7).

As a personal Father, God keeps His promises. Paul wrote to Titus, reminding the younger man that the former was:

> a servant of God and an apostle of Jesus Christ for the faith of God's elect and the knowledge of the truth that leads to godliness—a faith and knowledge resting on the hope of eternal life, which God, who does not lie, promised before the beginning of time (Titus 1:1,2).

As a personal Father, God is jealous for the love of His children. The only thing we know about jealousy is what we see of it in ourselves and in those around us. Our experiences of jealousy are enough to convince us that it is a cancerous and soul-destroying vice. How, then, can we say that God our heavenly Father is a jealous God? Does that not destroy our image of Him as the true and Holy God who has no part in sin and who cannot err?

God said this to Moses about the nation Israel entering the Promised Land:

Be careful not to make a treaty with those who live in the land where you are going, or they will be a snare among you. Break down their altars, smash their sacred stones and cut down their Asherah poles. Do not worship any other god, for the LORD, whose name is Jealous, is a jealous God (Exodus 34:12-14).

Paul the apostle, speaking of the compromising practices into which some early Christians had fallen by attending pagan feasts where sacrifices were being made to idols, warned against the absurdity and peril of such action when he asked, "Are we trying to arouse the Lord's jealousy?" (1 Corinthians 10:22).

James tells us that, "the spirit he [God] caused to live in us tends toward envy" (James 4:5). The Father jealously desires the relationship which He has designed between Himself and His children. He is zealous to protect that love relationship.

Human jealousy is a vicious evil to be feared. The Proverbs writer asks, "who can stand before jealousy?" (Proverbs 27:4) But the jealousy of men and the jealousy of God are two different things. Man's jealousy is vicious and destructive. God's jealousy is righteous and constructive. It may be asked how jealousy can be a virtue in God, yet a vice in men.

The reason for our dilemma is that we must employ human language to describe the characteristics of God our Father. Scripture is full of anthropomorphisms where human features are attributed to God (God's arm, hand, fingers, hearing, sight, anger, joy, and so on). All we have at our disposal are words, the tools of communication men use to describe each other. We must remember, however, that man is not and never could be the measure of his Maker. Attempts to describe God using human language always require greater qualification.

Just as God's wrath is not a reference to bad temper in God, so jealousy in God must not be thought of as the infantile resentment so often displayed in human nature. Human jealousy is the offspring of coveting. That is, human jealousy implies "I want what you've got and I hate you because I can't have it"— while jealousy in God always means a righteous and zealous attitude on God's part to protect the love relationship He desires between Himself and His children.

God's attitude toward unfaithfulness in His people is better appreciated when we realize that His faithfulness and righteousness demand unqualified love and loyalty (see Ezekiel 16:35-39). By telling Moses that His name is Jealous, God meant that He demands from His loved ones absolute loyalty. God's jealousy speaks of His covenant-keeping love, which will always respond to unfaithfulness by stern action designed to protect and preserve the intimacy of His family.

During the intertestamental period—that time spanning the end of the Old Testament age and the beginning of the New Testament era—men believed that God was out of their reach. God was thought to be so transcendent as to be too far from the affairs of men. It was believed that God was disinterested in the affairs of men and that He could not be approached with any confidence. So far had men strayed from a knowledge of God!

Now we know differently—just as the Prophets knew and the Psalmist testifies so regularly. Our God, our heavenly Father, is both personal and within the reach of His children. In fact, He has shown us that even when our reach seems too short, His is always long enough. He has never retracted His outstretched arms from His people.

That is our heavenly Father. Ever personal, ever near. A knowledge of His presence motivates us to say, "I am so glad I know Him!"

1. See Genesis 35:2. For a well-developed statement on the Names of God, see the article by the late G. T. Manley in *The New Bible Dictionary* (Grand Rapids: Wm. B. Eerdmans Publishing Co., 1962), pp. 478ff.

2. For further reading on the names of God, please see *Titles of the Triune God*, by Herbert F. Stevenson (Westwood, N.J.: Fleming H. Revell Co., 1956).

3. G. F. Moore, *Judaism*, vol. II (Cambridge: Harvard University Press, 1954), pp. 203-204.

8

FINDING FOLLOWS SEEKING

I stepped from the pulpit and made my way through the dispersing crowd in the direction of the auditorium's side door. As I proceeded, a young woman touched me on the arm and said with a smile, "I have something here which I have been wanting to give you for weeks." She pressed a note into my hands and with a nod of contentment that showed her task was complete, the young woman stepped aside. "Thank you," I said, continuing my exit.

Once home, the note came immediately to mind. I took it out and began to read. This was a significant moment indeed! The things which I believed were central in our relationship with God as Father were coming about in the life of this young woman. She wrote:

> I just want to thank you for your constant emphasis on God as our Father. I have always struggled to accept the love of the Father. You see, I have never really known a dad. Because of your constant emphasis on this point, I think that in spite of everything that's happened to me . . . the things you have been teaching us have comforted me, encouraged me and have been drawing me close to our Lord. Thank you . . .

Knowing the Father is the essence of life (see John 17:1-3). Until someone has been introduced to the Father, true life, true comfort, and real encouragement will remain unknown. Jesus Christ, God's Son, came into the world to

117

reveal the Father, to make Him known. By faith, the Christian has been introduced to the Father through the liberating action of the Son of God. The doors to God's household have been flung open and we have access into the grace of God our Heavenly Father. Paul assured the Christians in Rome of this very fact when he wrote:

> Therefore, since we have been justified through faith, we have peace with God through our Lord Jesus Christ, through whom we have gained access by faith into this grace in which we now stand. And we rejoice in the hope of the glory of God (Romans 5:1,2).

The Bible does not set out to prove the existence of God. His existence is assumed. Rather, the Bible suggests the exciting possibility of *knowing* God. It was God Himself who spoke through the prophet Jeremiah to declare:

> "Let not the wise man boast of his wisdom
>   or the strong man boast of his strength
>   or the rich man boast of his riches,
> but let him who boasts boast about this:
>   that he understands and knows me,
> that I am the LORD, who exercises kindness,
>   justice and righteousness on earth,
>   for in these I delight"
>   (Jeremiah 9:23,24).

When Paul was at Athens in Greece, he spent time reasoning and disputing with the Epicurean and Stoic philosophers whose philosophical meanderings had led them up and down the pathways of intellectual debate . . . but no closer to the living God. They brought the apostle to the Council of the Areopagus where he was to speak. Having examined their objects and idols of worship, he addressed them.

> Men of Athens! I see that in every way you are very religious. For as I walked around and observed your objects of worship, I even found an altar with this inscription: TO AN UNKNOWN

GOD. Now what you worship as something unknown I am going to proclaim to you.

The God who made the world and everything in it is the Lord of heaven and earth and does not live in temples built by hands. And he is not served by human hands, as if he needed anything, because he himself gives all men life and breath and everything else. From one man he made every nation of men, that they should inhabit the whole earth; and he determined the times set for them and the exact places where they should live. God did this so that men would seek him and perhaps reach out for him and find him, though he is not far from each one of us. "For in him we live and move and have our being." As some of your own poets have said, "We are his offspring."

Therefore since we are God's offspring, we should not think that the divine being is like gold or silver or stone—an image made by man's design and skill (Acts 17:22-29).

The inscription was "TO AN UNKNOWN GOD." In all their groping and philosophizing they had come no closer to knowing God. He remained, for them, unknown—and as far as they were aware, unknowable. He seemed—

> *beyond touch*
> *out of reach*
> *unapproachable*

Like the Moslem who cannot dare to think of God as Father because that would bring Him into the reach of men, because it would cause a man to become familiar with God, because it would cause God to draw close to a man—so the Stoic saw God as out of range.

The Stoic philosopher has nothing of which to boast!

The Moslem has nothing in which to rejoice!

The lost son of God (the sinner) has nothing to celebrate. Why? Because none of them know God: "Let him who boasts boast about this: that he understands and knows me," says the Lord.

Boast and You Shall Praise

Boast? Can it be possible that I am given the freedom to boast? Is it not wrong for a man or woman or young person to boast? Should I not suppress such expressions of delight? No. Not in the present context, at least. To boast of a knowledge of God is to praise loudly. It is to praise God uproariously.

What is the reason for such loud yells of praise and thanksgiving?

The reason is that "I know God!" What better reason could there be to sing for joy in worship and praise? God Himself gives His own endorsement to such expressions of heartfelt delight; but the one who does not know God will never have to suppress such feelings of delight. He will remain separated from that joy.

The philosophers whom Paul encountered described the living God as an unknown, unknowable deity. Modern philosophers have gone several steps further; they say He does not even exist. But their theories are akin to the parasites we learn about in biology class. The flatworm and tapeworm are insidious creatures that get into the digestive system, where they fasten onto the wall of an animal's intestines. There they spread themselves throughout the intestinal system, drawing all nutrient goodness from the animal and causing disease. Modern theories of philosophy (like those of Camus and Sartre) have spread their influence like tapeworms throughout the educational systems and philosophical debates of our time. They claim life is absurd, or at best a bad joke. Life, they say, is without meaning. Nothing has serious worth.

The same foundation supported both ancient and modern philosophers (which is really no foundation at all). Both refuse to recognize God as God. This disease of unbelief is the age-old scourge of sin, which renders a person both spiritually sick and blind. Man's pursuit of knowledge has only led him to ignore or deny true knowledge, because to refuse knowledge of God the Father is to remain ignorant of life as it truly is and was always meant to be.

Men like Camus and Sartre are correct in assessing life *as they see it* to be absurd, because what they define as "life" is really the death which man exchanged for life when he reversed the order of things by trying to live as a god rather than for God (see Romans 1:18-25).

Ignorance of God is ultimate ignorance.

Ignorance of the Father is ignorance of eternal life.

A knowledge of the Father is cause for loud praising because eternal life is wrapped up in that knowledge. In His prayer to the Father, Jesus brought it all down to grassroots for us when He said: "Now this is eternal life: that they may know you, the only true God, and Jesus Christ, whom you have sent" (John 17:3).

That knowledge involves a declaration of the Father's character—His holy love. Knowing these things is cause for loud praising. It is not the esoteric knowledge of certain heretics in early church history who delighted in their secret (and distorted) knowledge. This knowledge is public and accurate. It is to be told. Jesus has declared the Father publicly and openly—in His life, in His death, and in His resurrection. We do not have to grope for it in the dark like one may stumble for the light switch in the middle of the night. The light has come into the world. The Son has come, and the Father has been made known—but how does a man come to know God?

Seek and You Shall Find

No man comes to the Father unless he comes through the Son of God (see John 14:6). Yet if a man earnestly seeks to know God, he will find Him (see Matthew 7:7). In the Proverbs, we read God's own statement: "I love those who love me, and those who seek me find me" (Proverbs 8:17). The Psalmist speaks of the happiness which builds in the life of such a person when he says, "Blessed [happy] are they who keep his statutes and seek him with all their heart" (Psalm 119:2). God placed His own promise in the ears of his people through the words of Jeremiah the prophet: "You will seek me and find me when you seek me with all your heart" (Jeremiah 29:13).

King David understood the importance of seeking God. He was convinced that "finding" followed on the tail of "seeking," and that refusing to accept God after having found Him would spell eternal rejection.

Before the whole congregation of Israel David spoke to his son, who would inherit the responsibility of building the temple:

> And you, my son Solomon, acknowledge the God of your father, and serve him with wholehearted devotion and with a willing mind, for the LORD searches every heart and understands every motive behind the thoughts. If you seek him, he will be found by you; but if you forsake him, he will reject you forever (1 Chronicles 28:9).

Now, that is very interesting. The promises in Scripture and statements like David's tell us that if a person seeks God, he will find God. We are nowhere told that our seeking *may* result in finding—never encouraged to seek God *in the hope that* we may stumble upon a personal knowledge of Him. No, the Scriptures assure us that if we seek God diligently, we will find Him. And even more astoundingly—the Bible says that it is not only possible to seek God, but that God desires to be found. Our heavenly Father wants to be sought, longs to be known, yearns to be found. Why? Because He desires His family.

It is sometimes said of people that "they are really seeking for something"; it is implied they are seeking for God. It is possible for a young person to seek this "something" over many years, and finally be no closer to ending his confused state. Yet it is still said of him that he is seeking something, with the suggestion that it is God he is searching for.

How are we to interpret the young person's "seeking"? That he is seeking cannot be denied. But that he is seeking God can be most strongly doubted. Why? Because the Scriptures deny the possibility of someone's seeking God without finding Him. The young person may be seeking, but he is not seeking God.

Honest evaluation will show that he is probably finding everything else along the way *except* God—free love, drugs, philosophies that pamper man's own ego, gurus, meditation, even the occult. In other words, the person who is "seeking," but never finds God, is not seeking God. He is intent upon finding everything except God.

The reason, of course, is that he does not wish to find God. God's ways are too straight, too obvious, and usually deemed too restrictive and binding. Having interpreted God-centered living as too controlling, he wants to escape the control of God. As a result, he becomes bound up in the gripping forces of ungodliness. He remains a stranger to God and estranged from God. Yet in the face of it all, the words of God spoken by the prophet continue to call out:

> Seek the LORD while he may be found;
>   call on him while he is near.
> Let the wicked forsake his way
>   and the evil man his thoughts.
> Let him turn to the LORD, and he will have mercy
>   on him,
>   and to our God, for he will freely pardon.
>   (Isaiah 55:6,7)

The Marriage of "Seeking" and "Drawing"

Every believer, at some time in their pre-Christian experience, seeks God with a fervor whose enthusiasm is difficult to explain. Why does a person, having no background in church or the Bible or Sunday school or Christianity, begin to seek God? How do we explain the hungering in a heart which drives someone to a relentless search for God? The Scriptures give us a very clear explanation. In fact, the Son of God Himself explained: "No one can come to me unless the Father who sent me draws him, and I will raise him up at the last day" (John 6:44). God is at work to draw men and women and young people unto Himself—to bring them to recognize their need of Him.

Paul told the Christians in Rome that, "God's kindness

leads you toward repentance" (Romans 2:4).

Surgio had escaped in the night. His plane limped across the waters with one engine out of action. Just the thought of returning to the country which was gradually fading in the distance brought a wave of anxiety. To live in a communist country was, in Surgio's estimation, the most life-draining experience a man can know. He was not a believer, but he was convinced of the soul-destroying forces at work in the communistic ideologies which pervaded the country he loved but was leaving behind.

His search for reality in the midst of demoralizing influences had driven Surgio to flee. He hoped to find what he had always dreamed freedom to be. The plane, miraculously maintained in the air, eventually landed in the West, touching down upon a new beginning for this refugee and stranger to the Western world. Astronomy and astrology, astro-travel and various forms of occult worship had all figured in the experience of this man who sought to escape the chains of communistic domination.

Now he was in the West. Surely reality, meaning, and freedom would all combine to give him what his heart had longed for during the past years of barrenness and lifelessness.

When I met Surgio, he was in Australia. He spoke reasonably good English and walked with a confidence that can only be appreciated by those who have escaped into freedom out of a political strait-jacket. What stood out more than anything, however, was his smile. It seemed to stretch from his right ear, across his face and up to the lobe of his left ear. His white teeth were unmistakable symbols of a joy which ran deep. When he spoke, it was no longer as a refugee from a communist land, but rather as an excited child of God who had found not only political freedom, but new life in Christ.

The events which had led to his salvation and consequential joy, he related with the enthusiasm of a young child freshly come from Disneyland for the first time. This part of his story begins in Sydney, the capital city of New South Wales, on the lower east coast of Australia.

Looking out through his dark brown eyes, and smiling that luminous smile, he began.

A young man who spoke my language was in Sydney, standing at a point along Pitt Street. He was waiting for the ride which would conduct him several hundred miles across Australia to the city of Perth, where he expected to find work. While he waited, another man approached him (having recognized him as being from our country) and handed him a New Testament printed in our particular dialect.

As an aside, he added, "I didn't even know that such a rare book existed." Continuing the story, Surgio began to get quite excited:

In the meantime, I was working in an industrial settlement—a mining town—north of Perth, as a cook in the kitchen of the settlement. I shared a small hut with another worker, who told me that he was expecting a friend to arrive from the east coast during the next few days.

Surgio looked delighted at the thought of what he was telling me. "That friend would turn out to be the man in transit from Sydney," he said. "Within a few more days, the visitor arrived and I allowed him to use my bunk until he needed to move on."

The visiting young man placed the Bible on the table, where it sat untouched. Within a day or so, our visitor heard of other work and found a new ride north. Before dashing out, he expressed his thanks and told me I could keep the book that someone had given him on the street in Sydney. I thanked him, picked up the book, and discovered it was a Bible. I had never seen one before. God was bringing things together in my life. I had been searching for reality. I had been desperately longing to know if there was something or someone behind the stars that I loved to study—but I was totally ignorant of God.

Surgio spoke now with intensity and the conviction that God's actions toward him were no less than the overtures of His Fatherly love, drawing him to repentance and faith. He continued:

> I read the whole New Testament in a couple of days. It was impossible to put down. I would rush back from my kitchen duties and begin again to soak up the words of Scripture that were becoming so delightfully satisfying to my thirsty heart and soul and mind. Then, one night, having read the whole New Testament, I went outside (as was my custom) to lie down on the grass and to look up at the stars—and my life was turned around. As I lay there, the words of Scripture came repeatedly to my mind. For years I had looked up at the night sky from my horizontal vantage point and wondered—"Is there anyone there? Who is behind all this?" Now I saw it! It all came together in my mind and my heart and my soul. I cried out, "Yes! The God of the Bible. You are God. You are Lord of it all. You are the living God and I can know You. Praise be to God forever!" Without speaking to any person, there in the wilderness of Western Australia, under the stars, I came to a saving knowledge of God my Heavenly Father and His Son Jesus Christ, whom I trusted as my Lord and Master and Savior from sin.

Surgio experienced the marriage of seeking and drawing. There came a time in his life when he saw that the seeking which had typified his "journey" was closely linked with the drawing activity of God in his life.

My wife's experience is similar. She spoke to no one, but simply responded to the drawing of God as He moved in her life and through her experiences to bring her to Himself. It was some time later before either came to grips with much of the Scriptural teachings which are usually associated with evangelism. But regardless of the manner in

126

which God the Father chooses to call His children out of the world, two things remain constant. One is the promise that if a person truly seeks after God, God will be found. The second is that in the case of every single believer, God has been at work to draw that person unto Himself.

A double-headed question remains, however. Why does God allow Himself to be sought, and why does He draw His children to Himself?

God Desires to Be Found

When God our Father spoke of the new covenant He was going to make with His people, He made clear His desire that His children *know* Him. We read:

> "The time is coming," declares the LORD,
>   "when I will make a new covenant with the house of Israel
>   and with the house of Judah.
> It will not be like the covenant
>   I made with their forefathers
> when I took them by the hand
>   to lead them out of Egypt,
> because they broke my covenant,
>   though I was a husband to them,"
>   declares the LORD.
> "This is the covenant I will make with the house
>   of Israel
>   after that time," declares the LORD.
> "I will put my law in their minds
>   and write it on their hearts.
> I will be their God,
>   and they will be my people.
> No longer will a man teach his neighbor,
>   or a man his brother, saying, 'Know the LORD,'
> because they will all know me,
>   from the least of them to the greatest,"
>   declares the LORD.
> "For I will forgive their wickedness
>   and will remember their sins no more."
>   (Jeremiah 31:31-34).

God allows Himself to be sought and found. He draws men to a knowledge of Himself because He longs for the family He planned from eternity.

We cannot know the Father, however, apart from the heart-shaping ministry of the Holy Spirit. God has given His Spirit to His children as a reminder that the Father abides with us (see 1 John 4:13). The words of our Lord Jesus indicate that when the Spirit reveals to someone who Jesus is, that person will know the Father.

> But when he, the Spirit of truth, comes, he will guide you into all truth. He will not speak on his own; he will speak only what he hears, and he will tell you what is yet to come. He will bring glory to me by taking from what is mine and making it known to you. All that belongs to the Father is mine. That is why I said the Spirit will take from what is mine and make it known to you (John 16:13-15).

The Holy Spirit enables each believer to become part of God's family by explaining who Jesus is. Through Jesus the Father is made known. In coming to the hearts of men and women with the conviction of sin and righteousness and judgment (see John 16:8-11), the Holy Spirit reaches down into the depths of a man's being and there implants a knowledge of the Father's requirements for family members.

It is the Holy Spirit of God who breathes the family heartbeat into the Christian's breast and who appropriates the saving work of the Son at the cross of Calvary, so that the Christian might enter into the household of God's family and there know and enjoy the Father. Having found the Father, we look back along the path we have come and realize that He was drawing us from the start. With David, we can sing:

> Give thanks to the LORD, call on his name;
> make known among the nations what he has
> done.

Sing to him, sing praise to him;
    tell of all his wonderful acts.
Glory in his holy name;
    let the hearts of those who seek the LORD
    rejoice.
Look to the LORD and his strength;
    seek his face always.

    (1 Chronicles 16:8-11)

CHAPTER
9

SHOWING PRECEDES KNOWING

Three experiences rank among the most exciting and fulfilling of my life. While they shared definite similarities, each was distinctive and unique. Each was breathtaking and altogether overwhelming. Each afforded me a glimpse of the absolute beauty of God's love and perfection. But not one of them can ever be repeated.

I refer to the birth of each of our three daughters. So many of us have enjoyed the same thrill in the past, or will in the future. The excitement of being awakened in the early hours of the morning with the news, "Darling, I think it's time!" Rushing around for the appropriate attire and hoping that in the darkness you have indeed grabbed a matching pair of shoes!

I well recall the birth of our first daughter, Cammie. My mother-in-law has not forgotten that in my apparent calm and collectedness, I rushed to the car that morning carrying the baby basket—to the laughing shrieks of herself and my very expectant wife. It was hardly likely that in a country where women usually remain in the hospital for between seven and ten days after giving birth that we would be needing the basket just yet.

Our journey to the hospital took the best part of an hour. Alerted to our pending arrival, the nursing staff was at the ready. Margo, my wife, was admitted quickly with the gentleness that only personalized care could guarantee. There in that place, amid the sounds accompanying birth, life dawned upon our first child. Before the eyelids of time closed upon another day, we were parents.

How could we ever forget it? Here before our eyes was the shape of a tiny person whose character was yet to be developed, her little body suspended in the gloved hands of the doctor. Still attached to her mother by the umbilical cord, this brand new member of the Law family had not yet grappled with the reality of going solo.

With each of our daughters, the moment came when the doctor handed me the sterilized surgical cutters and I severed the little baby once and for all from her internal haven. Each one of the girls immediately voiced her disapproval by waving her arms about and yelling for air; but there was nothing she could do. As I held each of those tiny little people in the warm water provided to ease her transition from the security of the womb into a new environment, she decided it probably wasn't so bad after all. In fact, all three decided to stay, and we still have them, for which we praise God.

When the Lord Jesus, the Son of God, was born into the world, the cord was cut much sooner—it was when Mary became pregnant with the child of whom the prophet spoke in Isaiah 9:6. God severed the cord which had eternally secured His Son in the embrace of His Father ... letting Him loose into a hostile world. Yet Jesus the Son never voiced His disapproval.

He came willingly.

He came with a purpose.

He came to explain the Father ... to make the Father known.

The Abstract Made Concrete

So much about the Father seems abstract. So much appears beyond one's reach. A man was just putting some finishing touches on the driveway he had spent the day cementing, when a small boy came running along the footpath and stepped into the middle of the wet cement, spoiling the surface and many hours' work. The man was hopping mad and chased after the boy. He caught the youngster and boxed him around the ears. The man's wife, who had been watching from a window, saw the entire drama and called out to her spouse, "George, you were very rough on the boy! I thought you liked children!" Indignantly her husband replied, "I do. I like them in the abstract, but not in the concrete!"

The Lord Jesus reveals the Father in concrete terms. And He does so in order that we can know Him. Just as the oldest son in a Hebrew family would represent his father before the family whenever the father was absent, so Jesus, God's only begotten Son, represents the Father in the world where the Father is not physically visible. For that very reason, Jesus encouraged the disciples to pay close attention to His actions and words and to examine closely His attitudes. He said to Philip, "Don't you know me, Philip, even after I have been among you such a long time? Anyone who has seen me has seen the Father. How can you say, 'Show us the Father'?" (John 14:9). In the Lord Jesus the Father is made known, is shown, is revealed.

Now, if Jesus represents the Father before you and me, if His characteristics are essentially the same as the Father's, yet He remains the Son, how can Isaiah speak of this child who would be born as the *Everlasting Father*? (Isaiah 9:6).

Within Eastern cultures it is common for a very wise man, for example, to be called "The father of wisdom," or for a very foolish man to be called "The father of folly." The Lord Jesus is both eternal and the Father of eternal qualities which reveal not only Himself but also the character of our heavenly Father.

In sending His only begotten Son, God sent a living description of Himself—a perfect description which would never be spoiled or overshadowed by the conduct of the Son. As the One who perfectly describes the Father, the Lord Jesus Christ exhibited the eternal qualities of truth, peace, and life.

Jesus Shows the Father's Truth

Pilate asked Jesus, "What is truth?" even while the unblemished embodiment of Truth stood before his very eyes—the Lord Jesus Christ Himself.

John said of Jesus, "The Word became flesh and made his dwelling among us. We have seen his glory, the glory of the One and Only, who came from the Father, full of grace and truth" (John 1:14).

Jesus said of Himself, "I am the way and the truth and the life. No one comes to the Father except through me" (John 14:6). In other words, He said "I am the Way to the Father! I am the Truth pertaining to the Father! I am the Life of the Father!"

The greatest truth that anyone can ever possess is to know God as his or her personal heavenly Father. A knowledge of that truth is evidence of eternal life. Jesus prayed to the Father saying, "Now this is eternal life: that they may know you, the only true God, and Jesus Christ, whom you have sent" (John 17:3).

But I want you to be aware also that the greatest lie ever perpetrated by Satan is to convince people that he can adequately father them. He seeks to convince you and me of that very thing.

He whispered suggestions to Eve that "if you listen to me, I will take care of you. I have your best interests at heart. God is just trying to strait-jacket you with His rules . . ." He whispered to Jesus, "Bow down to worship me and I will give You everything you see before Your eyes . . ." He is still whispering today in his depraved, insidious way, "Do as I say and life will be pleasant for you . . . " all the while implying, "You can find your comfort in me! You do not need God the Father because I can adequately father you!"

What a lie! Our Lord summed this deceiver up perfectly when He said in effect, "You cannot believe a thing he says." Why? Because "when he lies, he speaks his native language, for he is a liar and the father of lies" (John 8:44). We need here to make an important observation. When God sent His Son into the world to display the Father, Jesus set His face toward the cross. There at Calvary the greatest battle that ever raged took place. It was a battle where the Eternal Father of Truth fought and defeated the father of falsehood, thus thwarting the lie forever.

The Truth Is Shown

God is Truth and Jesus came to declare that Truth. But what is truth? If truth is reality—that is, things as they really are, things as God intended them to be—then false-hood is things as they really are not; it is things that you have been enticed to believe, but which are not in fact real.

A Masquerade

Some friends arrived in the States from Australia, and I met them at the airport. These two young women had been in transit for some thirty hours, and they had no idea what waited for them that late evening hour as they stepped out of the concatenated walkway which conducted them from their airplane to our reunion. Their pastor of the last eight years, removed by one, was once again at their side; but things were not as they appeared. A masquerade was about to take place.

As we approached the luggage conveyer, I told them not to be overly concerned about the luggage since my chauffeur would take care of them. Each quickly looked at the other as if to register amazement that their pastor-student could possibly have said what they thought they had heard. But I continued talking to them as if I had not noticed.

In a matter of moments the chauffeur arrived, was in-troduced to the ladies, and began to load their luggage into the trunk of a magnificent, maroon colored Cadillac, the likes of which neither had seen before.

Shortly we were on our way, comfortably cruising along the six-lane freeway and surrounded by the lush cushion-ing of the limousine. The chauffeur continued to address me as "Sir" during our short trip through Portland, conduct-ing himself in a most business-like fashion. We turned into the grounds on which stood a beautifully kept mansion (a seminary, in fact) and were greeted at the large door by a butler, suitably dressed in swallow-tailed best.

Inside, a maid dressed in white cloth tiara and white apron met us and immediately ascended the internal stair-case to see if "Madame" (my wife) was ready to greet the guests. During these closing moments of the masquerade it was becoming apparent that our Australian visitors were bewildered. I could almost see the wheels churning: "Is this the same pastor we knew at home?" "Are we right to be sending financial support from our church in Australia for a man living in such economic comfort?" And so on.

Finally the truth was revealed.

"These are not my butler and maid," I confessed. "Greg is not my chauffeur and the car we have been enjoying tonight has been borrowed for the occasion. These are some of our friends who agreed to give you a never-to-be-forgotten 'landing' in America."

It was a joke, and it was fun. We all had a good and hearty laugh before going home to our more humble dwellings. But we have here a fitting illustration. What they saw and experienced were things as they really were not! Those trappings existed for that space of time only as a masquerade, a falsehood. The young women had been convinced to believe a lie: What they thought was true was really a sham. That is exactly what Satan, the father of lies, does. He masquerades as the Father of truth because he is a liar; and because he is a liar, he masquerades falsehood as truth.

The Truth Is Known

At Calvary's Cross, the Son of God emerged the Victor, declaring by His actions that:

> God *alone* is the true and living Father.
> He *alone* can comfort.
> He *alone* is worthy of our worship and is *altogether trustworthy*.

In a day when America has no less than three thousand cults with cultic leaders; in a day when false teachers abound and confused people flock to hear their words of apparent comfort, which only prove empty and hollow; in a day of gurus who convince men and women and young people that God is not Father—it is essential to return to the cross of Calvary and there be constantly renewed in the truth and certainty that God alone is able to be a Father to sinners. God alone can restore a sinner to His family.

Jesus Shows the Father's Peace

How do you define peace? If you were in war-ravaged Beirut, you might define peace as the absence of war. If you live in a home where people spend their time fighting, you may define peace as the absence of argument.

The second grade teacher at the school our children attend battles the learning difficulties of poor children who cannot learn because their home environment is so tense and unhappy that they are plagued to distraction. Peace may be defined by the broken-hearted school child as "the times Mommy and Daddy stop fighting."

During family devotions one morning we asked our children, "What do you have when two people argue?" After waiting a moment, one of the girls answered, "A war!" I thought that was rather insightful. But I do not wish here to define the peace of God in terms of war. Rather, I want to define *peace*—the peace which comes from God and is championed in the Lord Jesus Christ as the Eternal Father of peace—in four words. You may wish to add others, but I am limiting the definition to four. Peace, in God's view, is *the absence of anxiety.*

I picked up the telephone one morning and the voice at the other end sobbed, "We have lost everything. We need help . . . " Through the tears I could detect the heartache and anxiety of a family in desperate need.

Indelibly marked upon my memory is another evening when an anxious mother phoned to say that life had treated her so badly that she intended to end it all that night, for herself as well as her three children.

I cannot forget the bulimic whose closet "eating and then purging" lifestyle had bound her in its grip for years—she sat in a chair opposite mine, her eyes anxiously asking, "Who can possibly help me?"

I remember, too, the young man at whose side I stood after his fifth and almost successful attempt at suicide had left him drugged and temporarily without any consciousness of where he was or the results of what he had done. And I think back to the subsequent times of counsel as he battled with the inner turmoil that remained.

It is so easy to give glib answers at times like these. It's so easy to rattle off a collection of clichés worn threadbare through overuse. Yet one thing remains true regardless of time's passing: When the Lord Jesus promised the disciples peace, He said it would be like nothing else they had ever known. It would be a double-barreled peace, dispelling anxiety and dissolving fear. He told His devoted followers, who grew anxious and fearful at the thought of His leaving them:

> Do not let your hearts be troubled. Trust in God;
> trust also in me. In my Father's house are many
> rooms; if it were not so, I would have told you. I
> am going there to prepare a place for you. And if
> I go and prepare a place for you, I will come back
> and take you to be with me that you also may be
> where I am (John 14:1-3).

But how could He possibly say to these folk whose hearts were so disturbed by impending circumstances, "Do not let your hearts be troubled"? How? Because that peace, coming forth from the Father of peace, would be perfectly suited to every situation regardless of how insurmountable the odds may have appeared. Because it would be a peace given in the context of Father and child . . . a gift from the Father to His child.

The key issue for anyone consumed by anxiety is this: Belief in God as Father and the absence of anxiety are linked. They go together. Yet someone may still say, "That is all well and good, but they do not go together for me!" It may be that your only images of a father are negative, which puts God in a bad light. You may confess, "I am so angry at God because as a child I lived in fear of what my father might do to abuse me. I prayed earnestly, but God did not intervene to stop him. I am so hurt and angry and bitterly disappointed with God. Why didn't God intervene on my behalf?!"

The objection isn't inconsequential. Many young people are suffering today at the hands of an abusive earthly father— suffering cruelty, sexual abuse, and many other forms of mistreatment—to such an extent that their image of God as Father is wholly distorted. And I do not know why God did not intervene in your past to end your father's abuse, or why He did not keep your child from dying or prevent your business from failing or save your husband or wife from a painful death at the hands of cancer. No one can accurately explain why. We can theorize, given certain details—but we cannot really know *why*.

The Scriptures assure us that some of God's children shut the mouths of lions and quenched the power of fire; that some escaped the edge of the sword and from weakness were made strong; that some even received back their dead by resurrection. But the same Scriptures also assure us that others of God's children were mocked and scourged, chained and imprisoned . . . were stoned . . . and put to death by the sword (see Hebrews 11:32ff.).

We cannot tell why God intervenes on behalf of some and not for others. There is something, however, that we do know. We know that God remains the perfect Father and is still in total control. We know that He understands the hurt and the feelings of guilt and anger in a way that only He as our gracious Father in heaven can do; and that He is ready and waiting to apply the balm of Gilead in order to heal the wound. We know that His arms are outstretched and He longs to embrace you in His love and by His tender compassion. And we remain convinced that a belief in God as our Father—the kind of Father who far exceeds our wildest expectations and who can only be expressed as perfect— dispels all anxiety.

Why? Because there we are brought to see that God the Father is both personal and reachable; ever present, ever caring, never "out" to His children. The Psalmist tells us that. He writes of God: "As a father has compassion on his children, so the LORD has compassion on those who fear him" (Psalm 103:13). Moses expressed it this way: "The eternal God is your refuge, and underneath are the everlasting arms" (Deuteronomy 33:27a).

Dear friend, that is what the absence of anxiety is all about: *Knowing the Father's embrace.* That is what the Lord Jesus came to show as the One who is eternally the Father of peace.

Showing the Father's Life

Our family has spent many summer holidays on the edge of the Pacific Ocean, allowing the benevolence of sunshine and rest to pamper our weary bodies in readiness for another twelve months of work. To many Australians, life entails "sun, surf, and sand." For them, there can be no other definition. For an Oregonian who likes sun, life is probably best defined as "early June to late August."

Regardless of how you define life, one thing can be stated definitively from the words of Jesus: Without a knowledge of God the Father, it is impossible to live. Praying to the Father, Jesus said, "Now this is eternal life: that they may know you, the only true God, and Jesus Christ, whom you have sent" (John 17:3). That is, in fact, why He came. Jesus said, "I have come that they may have life, and have it to the full" (John 10:10).

A relationship with God as Father is the only correct environment for life.

A Wrong Environment for Life

An illustration I heard once in another setting is appropriate here. Imagine you are on holiday and you have an apartment overlooking the sand and surf at Long Beach in California or Surfer's Paradise on Australia's Gold Coast. Sitting on the table in your lounge room is a fishbowl, and inside the bowl is a small goldfish. Each day you swim and sun-bake and enjoy soaking up the delights of vacationing. Before long, however, you begin to feel sorry for little Goldie who is all alone in his bowl while you go out having fun in the sun. In an effort to make up for this injustice you promise Goldie a little of the action. "Tomorrow," you tell the goldfish, "you will begin to enjoy life too."

The next day you take a washcloth, lift the fish from the bowl, place it in the cloth, wrap it up, and put the living bundle into your pocket before leaving for the beach.

As you reach the spot where you are accustomed to spending your day, you can feel the sun's heat beating down upon your back. Excitedly you take your gilled companion from your pocket, lay out the washcloth on the sand, place the fish on the cloth, stand back, and say, "Now this is the life, Goldie; live it up!"

Can anything be more ridiculous or more foolish? Being in the sun on the hot beach is no environment for a goldfish—or any fish! It will die there, not live. It was never intended to be in that environment.

Jesus told a similar story recorded by Luke (Luke 15:11-32), the story of the prodigal son who came to his father and said in essence, "I am tired of being hemmed in by this environment. I don't want to be a part of this household any longer. Give me my inheritance and set me free to go my own way." He resigned from the family and left, turning his back not only on the family but also on his father. Soon his money, friends, and parties had all dissipated. He was left alone, penniless and hungry. He found himself working in a pigsty, where the pangs of hunger urged him to fill his stomach with the pigs' leftovers.

While he sat among that band of bacon chums, something happened. It was as if a blind was rolled up to let the light in on his understanding. He remembered his father and his home. He realized that he was now pitiful, wallowing in the wrong environment. There he sat, having lost all dignity—reduced to a companion of pigs.

This revelation of home penetrated deeply into his mind, activating his sense of self-respect. He said, "I will return to my father to become a hired servant, since even the servants are doing better than I am right now." So he began his journey home. As he approached that familiar setting, he saw a figure in the distance looking down the road in his direction. It was his father, the same father who had watched daily in the hope of his son's return. The scene must have been moving indeed.

The moment his father was certain that his prodigal had come home, he ran to meet him, his heart bursting with emotion at the joy of answered prayer. As the two met, father and son face-to-face, the latter cried, "Father, I have sinned against heaven and against you. I am no longer worthy to be called your son . . ." He was about to add, ". . . make me like one of your hired men," but he never finished. His father's embrace was far too overwhelming, his actions too forgiving, and his intentions far too restorative. The father's actions spoke a loud message. It was as if he said, "Do not come home to ask what you can do for me. You do not have to work your way back into my favor or into my affections." The father loved his son, he forgave him; he embraced him and restored him to life in the family. He restored him to the correct environment.

The Father Needs to Act

The prodigal son came to an understanding of his father, home, and family in the midst of a foreign environment—the pigsty. But what needs to be pointed out is that no man will ever come to a revelation of God the Father on his own, regardless of the surroundings in which he finds himself. It was necessary for God the Father to act on behalf of lost sons.

Now, that is precisely what God did! He sent the Lord Jesus Christ, His only Son, into a hostile environment to retrieve you and me. The One who is eternally the Father of life came to reveal the Father to us where we were. It was the supreme desire of God the Father to have sons and daughters who would glorify Him through their loving obedience to His Word and humble service in His household.

To know the Father is to love Him. To be His child is to resemble Him. As a child of God, you are loved on the basis of the Son of God's sacrificial death, not on account of individual gifts or abilities or personal merits. Each is equally loved by the Father and Son; there are no favorites in the family. All are equal in status since all have had to be redeemed, purchased back, from a state of sin in which each failed to glorify, honor, and serve God out of loving devotion.

Just as the prodigal son could not accurately represent his father or family while outside the boundaries of the father's embrace, so the sinner is in no position to glorify the Father until restored to his family. Having been restored to the Father—to family, to dignity, and to life—we serve Him out of willing desire. Not only so, but we look forward to the day when we will see Him face to face.

The Son Has Come to Show

Some time ago, our middle daughter came home very excited about a plan she had cooking. Heading for my study door and gaining entrance, she asked, "Daddy, will you come with me next Wednesday?"

"Where to, sweetheart?" I asked.

"To the girls' club," she replied. Since I was not in the habit of attending girls' club, I was most curious and could not think why she would want me there. So I asked: "Why, darling?"

Her answer stumped me. "*Because I want to Show and Tell you!*"

Have you ever been the object of "Show and Tell"? In the passage we began with in Isaiah 9:6, the prophet writes, "For to us a child is born, to us a son is given." Why? Why did Jesus come? Why did God the Father send the Son? In order that He might Show and Tell the Father!

I am so comforted by the thought that God initiated that move toward sinners—toward me. I needed Him to move in my direction and to confront me with Himself. Only in glimpsing His holiness and experiencing His grace, only in discovering the truth concerning His status and authority, could I have ever turned away from sin with the conviction of my need and convinced of His grace.

When I gaze upon the Lord Jesus, I am assured of my sin. Only when I gaze upon Jesus am I convinced that I am undeserving. Yet when I rest my eyes upon the One whose arms are outstretched to me in an open display of the Father's holiness and forgiving love, my eyes well up with tears of joy and I cry out with John Newton of old, *Amazing Grace!*

How very beautiful to be the recipients of the Father's grace. The Lord Jesus has shown us the Father! Now He says to each of us: "Do you understand what it is that I am offering you? Do you realize what the Father is seeking to do through My disclosure of His character? Let Me show you. I am offering you the truth so that you can turn away from Satan's lie. I am exposing the masquerade so that you can turn away from things as they really-are-not. I am offering you peace from guilt and anxiety, so that you no longer need to run and hide from the Father. I am offering you life, as a child of God."

One thing remains to be said, and our Lord Himself said it. If you are to come to the Father, if you are to embrace truth and peace and life as God has designed it and intended it for His children, then says our Lord Jesus, "You will have to come through Me because there is no other route, no detour, no alternatives."

Having received God's gracious favor and having become His child, I will be alerted to my true identity every time I pray. Why? Because I will be confident that my Father in heaven is concerned enough to listen, to answer, to advise, to chasten, challenge, encourage, or instruct me. Each time I feel depressed or lonely, isolated or deserted, I will be reminded that my Father is close at hand, always ready to hear me out. Above all, I will rejoice in knowing that I have been restored to the family from which my sin had severed me, and that my Heavenly Father cared enough to send His only begotten Son in search of such family casualties as I.

The sense of personal delight in knowing all this is conveyed in the following declaration of . . .

A Son's Joy

. . . O how I love my Father, whose hand stretched out to me,
A lonely, lost and rebel son who brought Him agony.
To think that from His heavenly home all glorious and
resplendent,

The Son would come to rescue one who sought for independence.

I see a glimpse of Father God in what His hand created;
I think I see a glimpse in men, or are they unrelated?
But, when I look upon the Son, and fix my gaze, I rather . . .
Fancy that in Him I see a perfect view of Father.

The Word came down and dwelt among us, full of grace and
truth;
Witness to the glorious God who made both earth and
heaven.
And in His face aglow with light, the source of life I see . . .
A gift from Father's caring heart to sinners such as me.

My Father now has ceased to be a stranger in my life;
And as a child of God I know I am where I ought to be.
Within the Household of my God, an orphan nevermore.
Since by His grace He rescued me, to love Him evermore.
    Amen.

10

ADOPTION IS NOT AN OPTION

It was 10:00 P.M. A crowd had gathered outside gate 38. Excitement buzzed through the air and conversations ran on a high note of expectation. The airport corridor had become the waiting place for the family and friends of a young couple returning to the United States from Colombia. We had come to meet Margo's parents, who were arriving from Australia on the same flight. My family stood watching the much larger group, which provided us a source of interest while we waited.

Very soon we were discussing the reason for their collective effervescence with some of the people standing about. The young couple due in from Colombia had left the States a week or so earlier, as two. They were returning as a family of five. They had adopted two little boys and a little girl in South America, and would soon step through the gate from the aircraft having become an instant family. Excited hearts were beating within the "instant" grandparents, "instant" uncles and aunts, and "instant" friends of the newly formed family.

In no time we were as excited as the rest, as expectant of the arrival of this new family as that of our own. Stepping into view, the newly formed family unit was met by the cheers of the waiting crowd. There was not a disappointed heartbeat in that whole section of the airport. For the children, a new life had begun in the household of their

American father. They had been secured. They would be loved. They would take on the privileges of being part of that family—and all because they had been adopted.

Adoption calls to mind different things to different people. A person who has been disappointed in his adopted home will probably think negatively about adoption. The child who has been reared in a loving adopted family will delight in the term and in its connotations. Parents who have had a long and constant struggle with an adopted child may well be cautious about recommending adoption to a younger couple.

In the first half of this twentieth century (in Australia at least), the public's attitude toward adoption was negative. My own parents' experience bears that out. My older brother and sister were both adopted into our family at a time when it appeared that my mother would not be able to have children of her own. But it was not until these two children had grown that my parents felt free to declare their adoption. Previously they hesitated because of the stigma which so often harassed adopted children and their families.

The modern approach, which has exposed the earlier attitudes as inhumane and brutal, is quite different. Now parents are encouraged to inform the child as early as possible of the adoption, and to explain the process as a special choice made by the parents—"We selected you because you were very special and we wanted you to be a part of our family."

You know, that is exactly what God our Heavenly Father has done! He has adopted us into His family and made us His own, despite the stigma. Jesus was berated by the Pharisees for sitting with publicans and sinners, but these were the very ones the Father intended to adopt into His family. There is not a Christian alive who has not been adopted; not a saint in heaven who was not adopted. You see, unless you are adopted, there is no possible way for you to enter into the family of God.

Adoption is not an option—it is not an alternative route to the Father's embrace. It is adoption, or it is nothing.

Prodigal Sons Need Adopting

Our plane sat on the tarmac. We were already late. Departure time departed without us, and the Chicago airport had lost any possible attraction for those of us who had flown in earlier from New York. The prospect of several more hours in the air did not appeal to me. I had a greater longing to finish the journey which had begun eight days before. Still we waited.

Suddenly from the front de-planing door appeared the face of a travel agent whose apologetic manner gave voice to his embarrassment at the delay. "We are over-booked on this flight," he informed us, the note in his voice promising a further suggestion. "The first six people to volunteer to leave the plane will receive $200 air travel credit with this airline, $100 cash in hand, and a first class seat on a later flight to the West Coast with all the alcohol you can drink." He waited confidently for the response. He had done this before.

It came within moments. People began to raise themselves from their seats and move to the front of the aircraft, indicating their willingness to make the "sacrifice." Amongst them were a number of red-clad young people—late 20s to early 30s—each wearing a long set of wooden beads with a photograph in a small wooden frame, attached where the pendant would normally be. I had seen them before . . . in airports, on flights, in the streets—but always in groups and always dressed in this uniform, faded red clothing.

Each one was a Sannyasin—a devotee of the Bhagwan Shree Rajneesh—bound for the ashram (commune) near the town of Antelope in eastern Oregon, now known as Rajneeshpuram. They would join many hundreds of devotees from as far away as Europe and Australia who were making the journey to Oregon for an international convention of the gurus' followers.

Each is a prodigal from God. Each has chosen a substitute god (*Bhagwan* means god) and has been deluded into thinking that this substitute could provide the family environment which only the true and living God can give. Each longs for adoption but is determined that it can be found in the wrong place. Each, in his prodigal state, ignores the living God, being attracted to the mind-raping philosophies of a mere man whose hold upon his devotees is coupled with a lifestyle which places no restraints whatever upon the extremes of human behavior. Floether writes of Rajneesh that he:

> ... leans heavily on the doctrine of the void. ... The purpose of his meditations, workshops, lectures, therapies and even sex groups is to bring about this state of emptiness, creating the mindless man. The mindless man is the enlightened man: he has no past, no future, no thought, no attachment, no mind, no ego, no self ..." [and he would add, no sin] " ... For those who seek enlightenment today, he points to himself. In an unabashed theft from the words of Christ, Rajneesh once remarked: "To them [my followers] I can say: 'I am a Master.' To them I can say: 'Come to me and drink out of me, and you will not be thirsty, ever.'"[1]

These red-clad devotees have pledged their lives to this self-appointed god. Having run from the true Father, they have been swept off their feet by the lie of idolatry. Theirs is idol worship. Their adoption is invalid—because the "father" is no father at all. They have forfeited true sonship and true familyhood in favor of delusion, the inevitable outcome of refusing to know God the Father. It is the consequence of man's desire for autonomy, for independence from God and His true family. They remain in desperate need of the adoption initiated and administered from heaven, an adoption which translates a person out of the kingdom of darkness into the kingdom of light, an adoption which rescues a lost son or daughter and returns him or her to the household of God.

The Prodigal Son of Luke 15 did not leave home because he had been rejected by his father and his family. No, the prodigal removed himself, turning his back on his father and family. He rejected home and went in search of fulfillment elsewhere. Actually, he went in search of what he already had; he simply failed to recognize that he already had it. Humanly speaking, the only true fulfillment that a father can have is to be surrounded by the glory of his family.

Humanly speaking, the only fulfillment a son can have in life is to be embraced by father and family. God created us to be sons—His sons. He designed us to work best in a family—His family. God, the Father, through whom every family on earth derives its name, has always intended that we live in harmony as His sons and daughters. He has always desired that we display His Fatherhood in our sonship and glorify Him as Father by our actions.

Sin originally enticed Adam away from the embrace of God so that he became a prodigal. Since that time every man and woman has been born in the prodigal state of sin. Therefore lives simply waste away outside the bounds of the true family. There, in isolation from Father and family, men will grope in vain for a substitute, suffering the effects of denied sonship.

From Foreigners to Family, by Adoption

How do we become members of God's family? This transition is accomplished through an act of grace on the part of God our Heavenly Father. Paul wrote about this:

> Therefore, remember that formerly you who are Gentiles by birth and called "uncircumcised" by those who call themselves "the circumcision" (that done in the body by the hands of men)— remember that at that time you were separate from Christ, excluded from citizenship in Israel and foreigners to the covenants of the promise, without hope and without God in the world. But now in Christ Jesus you who once were far away have been brought near through the blood of Christ.
>
> For he himself is our peace, who has made the two one and has destroyed the barrier, the

dividing wall of hostility, by abolishing in his flesh the law with its commandments and regulations. His purpose was to create in himself one new man out of the two, thus making peace, and in this one body to reconcile both of them to God through the cross, by which he put to death their hostility. He came and preached peace to you who were far away and peace to those who were near. For through him we both have access to the Father by one Spirit.

Consequently, you are no longer foreigners and aliens, but fellow citizens with God's people and members of God's household, built on the foundation of the apostles and prophets, with Christ Jesus himself as the chief cornerstone. In him the whole building is joined together and rises to become a holy temple in the Lord. And in him you too are being built together to become a dwelling in which God lives by his Spirit (Ephesians 2:11-22).

The Christian is no longer a stranger from home. He is no longer an alien. He has permanent status as a member of God's family, with access to the Father through the Holy Spirit. Frustration reigns in the heart of lost children because they limp about in a dislocated state. They must constantly endure the pain of being divorced from the core relationship around which the family of God revolves. If the familyhood of God's children is the offspring of His Fatherhood, then the dislocated child suffers the loss of both: No family and no father.

Yes, it is true that insofar as God has created all men, He is the Father of all men. But the message of the Scriptures is not a message of universal fatherhood, ignoring the intimacy of that relationship (into which we must enter by faith). On the contrary, the message of the gospel is one which stresses a personal relationship with the Father through the forgiveness of sins, and adoption into the family.

While God remains the Creative Father of all men, not

all men are the recreated children of God. Some are strangers to repentance and faith, and these are alien to the City of God. One writer says:

> when our Lord taught His disciples to say, "Our Father," He was . . . indicating a relationship with God into which He was bringing His disciples by grace through faith. Only the sons of God, through personal trust in Christ as their Savior, can, then, truly pray the Lord's Prayer—which has more fittingly been termed "the disciples' prayer."[2]

May I suggest that it might even more fittingly be called "the prayer of sons" who may now approach the throne of God's grace, saying, "Our Father." This very relationship is one which each child of God shares with every other child of God. This fellowship with the Father is something you share with all the elect, if indeed you are a recreated child of God. It is within this relationship that we are enabled to "grasp how wide and long and high and deep is the love" (Ephesians 3:18) of this new family setting into which we have been adopted.

Privileged Sons and Heirs, by Adoption

Are you excited about your sonship or daughterhood? If Westcott is right (and I believe he is) that the name *Father* is the "sum of Christian revelation,"[3] then the term *sonship* is the most delectable fruit of that revelation available to men. To partake of the sonship God the Father offers us in Christ Jesus our Lord is to enjoy the delights of heaven on earth. It is to walk in the company of men and women whose citizenship is in heaven and whose future is assured as fellow heirs with Christ, the Son of God.

Having received the right to become the children of God (see John 1:12), we cry out "Abba! Father!" because "the Spirit himself testifies with our spirit that we are God's children" (Romans 8:16). It is the Spirit of God Himself who convinces the Christian that he or she is a child of God. He speaks to my believing heart and assures me of my heavenly Father's endorsement. It is "because you are sons," writes Paul, that "God sent the Spirit of his Son into our hearts, the Spirit who calls out, 'Abba, Father!'" (Galatians 4:6).

Gifts for Adopted Children

As privileged children and heirs of the Father, conscious of His endorsement and acceptance, we may be confident in His presence, certain of His attention, and assured of His every good and perfect gift. Referring to this kinship between the Father and His children, as that relates to asking from the Father, Smail says:

> Where there is no assurance of the relationship with the Father, there cannot either be any great expectation about the operation of the Spirit and His gifts. The Spirit has to witness to us that we are sons before He can lead us into the possessions that belong to sons (Romans 8:16-17). In terms of Luke 11:13, it is only when we can approach God as a Heavenly Father who has accepted us and is willing to give His best to us, that we shall have the confidence of faith to ask Him for the gift or work of the Spirit that we need.[4]

The Father has many blessings in store for His children. He also loves to bestow them on us now, here, on earth. When God gifts His children, it is for the benefit of the whole family. The preaching gift of one son will encourage and challenge many, the hospitality of another will warm the hearts of others, the wisdom of yet another will bring guidance to a family member in need.

It is the Spirit of God who assures us that we are His children, who encourages us in the ways of holy living, who affirms and reaffirms to our hearts the reality of our eternal hope, and who works in us to will and to do the good pleasure of our Heavenly Father.

Furthermore, it is the Holy Spirit who directs our affections back to the Word of God as the authoritative ground of our faith, who implants in the child of God a hunger and a thirst for righteousness, who produces that fruit which is no less than the character of the Lord Jesus Christ in the life of God's children (see Galatians 5:22,23).

What greater gift could there be? John was excited about his sonship. He drew our attention to the wonders of it when he wrote, "How great is the love the Father has lavished on us, that we should be called children of God! And that is what we are!" (1 John 3:1).

Set Among Sons

Sonship brings with it the responsibilities of living as members of God's family. It is so good to know God as my Father, but I must live in such a way that no one would be tempted to deny my claim to family membership. The same Holy Spirit Who enables us to cry "Abba! Father!" is the Spirit who is at work in the life of each child of God to produce transformed patterns of behavior. Previous patterns, traced around sin's template, once identified the actions and lifestyle of each sinner as typical of a lost child—a prodigal whose family resemblance was so smudged and sullied by disobedience and rebellion as to be unrecognizable. Habitual sin has been replaced by holy living. John said it well:

> Dear friends, now we are children of God, and what we will be has not yet been made known. But we know that when he appears, we shall be like him, for we shall see him as he is. Everyone who has this hope in him purifies himself, just as he is pure.
>
> Everyone who sins breaks the law; in fact, sin is lawlessness. But you know that he appeared so that he might take away our sins. And in him is no sin. No one who lives in him keeps on sinning. No one who continues to sin has either seen him or known him.
>
> Dear children, do not let anyone lead you astray. He who does what is right is righteous, just as he is righteous. He who does what is sinful is of the devil, because the devil has been sinning from the beginning. The reason the Son of

God appeared was to destroy the devil's work.
No one who is born of God will continue to sin,
because God's seed remains in him; he cannot
go on sinning, because he has been born of God.
This is how we know who the children of God are
and who the children of the devil are: Anyone
who does not do what is right is not a child of
God; neither is anyone who does not love his
brother (1 John 3:2-10).

Having been set among the sons of God, I delight to
please my Father. To sin is no longer the habit of my life—it
is not the regular practice it once was. When I do sin, I have
an advocate (One Who pleads my case) with the Father.
That One is Jesus Christ the Son, my Savior and Lord—my
Brother (see Hebrews 2:11ff.). I am contented in the face of
life's struggles, knowing that despite the pain, the frustrations, the hurts which may come, nothing will separate me
from the love of my heavenly Father. You see, He demonstrated just how much He loves me by going out in search
of me when I was lost, and never giving up the search until
He found me. It gives me such assurance of the genuineness and the abiding nature of His love and affection toward me. Dr. Packer says it so succinctly:

If God in love has made Christians His children,
and if He is perfect as a Father, two things would
seem to follow, in the nature of the case. First,
the family relationship must be an abiding one,
lasting forever. Perfect parents do not cast off
their children. Christians may act the prodigal,
but God will not cease to act the prodigal's
father. Secondly, God will go out of His way to
make His children feel His love for them, and
know their privilege and security as members of
His family. Adopted children need assurance
that they belong, and a perfect parent will not
withhold it.[5]

I am so glad that I know Him as my Father! So thrilled
by the knowledge of my family status, thrilled with my

brothers and sisters in Christ with whom I can fellowship and amongst whom I can serve God! Together we are learning to enjoy those things which the Father enjoys, to grieve at the things which grieve Him and to jealously guard against anything which might damage that relationship into which He has brought us.

I want my life to reflect the glory of my heavenly Father, don't you? To so act that others will say, "He must be a son of God; she must be a daughter of God; they so resemble their Father!"

Set among sons. What a privilege! "Adopted through propitiation, to redeemed sonship."[6] Our hearts have a song to sing and to shout from every rooftop . . .

> Set among sons, the Father has moved to show
>   His love,
> Born from the world into life.
> When I was lost, bound up in my sin, a stranger
>   from home,
> God, in His love, brought me home.
> Loving the world, was always to be the thing for
>   me.
> But God in His love, brought me home.
> Loving my life, ignoring the Son and all He had
>   done,
> Showed hate for the Father alone.
>
> Set among sons, the only perfect Son
> Has come with good news of the Father, and His
>   love;
> There is a way, forgiveness to know,
> See Christ in your place on the tree.
> What manner of love is this,
> That we should be called the children of God.
> What manner of love is this,
> To walk with the living God?
>
> Set among Sons, the Father has moved to show
>   His love,
> Born from the world into life.

When I was lost, bound up in my sin, a stranger
   from home,
God in His love, brought me home . . .
That I might be . . . set among His sons.

1. Eckart Floether and Eric Pement, "Bhagwan Shree Rajneesh," in *A Guide to Cults and New Religions* (Downers Grove: InterVarsity Press, 1983), p. 53.

2. Herbert F. Stevenson, *Titles of the Triune God* (London: Fleming H. Revell, 1956), p. 97.

3. Ibid., p. 97.

4. Thomas A. Smail, *The Forgotten Father* (William B. Eerdmans Publishing Co., 1980), p. 137.

5. J. I. Packer, *Knowing God* (Downers Grove: InterVarsity Press, 1973), p. 204.

6. Ibid., p. 194.

To Know Him Is To Love Him

"God our heavenly Father
had one thing in mind from the very beginning:
to have children at His side, enjoying forever
the joy and delight of being a part of God's family."

CHAPTER
11

ON MY FATHER'S MIND

New Zealand is such a long way from Oregon. So too is Australia. Too wet to walk! Too far to swim! The long miles render family and friends out of sight, out of reach, out of touch—but never out of mind.

I had been away from my wife and daughters for three weeks. Twenty-one long days in Australia, with the prospect of another week in New Zealand; and I had missed them with increasing intensity since the day after I left behind the American shoreline. It was so good to be reunited with relatives, friends, and church family "down under." Yet my heart constantly tugged in the direction of the ones I love most dearly. To *pine* is to long with a yearning. I pined for my family in Oregon.

As the plane carrying me back to the States rushed through the air above the Tasman Sea, I occupied my time talking with the young people who sat at my side. Another twenty-seven hours in transit, and a reunion would dismiss the pain of being separated.

How hard it must be for the serviceman whose career can take him away from family for months at a time! How difficult for the prisoner locked away . . . for the bedridden confined to hospitals . . . for the divorced, the bereaved, the rejected of this world. The *pain* of isolation. How very real it is.

As a father, I know what it is to love my children—and as a father I know what it means to long for the embrace of children who are a vast Pacific Ocean away. That is a long stretch—but if I could have extended my arms the distance, I would have done it. There was so much to say, so much to share, so much to enjoy and tell about the trip back to Australia. But I had no family at my side with whom to share it.

Mark Twain said, "To get the full value of joy you must have somebody to divide it with." I had one thing on my mind: to get home to my family as quickly as possible, in order to divide the joy.

God our heavenly Father had one thing in mind from the very beginning: to have children at His side, enjoying forever the joy and delight of being a part of God's family. To share the joy of *family* with children whose lives reflect the glorious characteristics of their Father. To embrace the children upon whom He would daily lavish His fatherly attention, displaying before them and in them His great graciousness. The Father longed for His children to enjoy Him—forever—but something defaced that intention. Sin drove a wedge between God and His sons. They became absent, lost; and the Father longed for His wayward children.

The Overtures of the Father

I picked up the receiver in my hotel room and began to dial a number my friend had given me before I left home. "By all means call them," he had said enthusiastically, hoping that an encouraging word to parents in pain might bring some soothing. I had never met this couple. San Francisco and the Bay area is so extensive that my short stay would prevent me from visiting in person or talking at length about their personal dilemma. Someone answered. It was a woman's voice.

"Hello, can I help you?" She sounded bright and in good spirits.

"Yes, hello. My name is Peter and I am a friend of your son. He asked me to call you while I was down in your area to see how you were coping with the current crisis. Are you encouraged by the progress being made?"

"We certainly are, thank you," she replied. Realizing the

pause in our conversation was her cue to continue, she went on. "My husband is flying out today and is hoping that the investigations will turn up a positive lead on our daughter's whereabouts. There is a team of people waiting in another state, ready for the deprogramming which will be an essential part of the recovery process once Helen is rescued."

Helen, their daughter, was entrenched in one of America's estimated 3,000 cult groups. She'd been there for more than a year. She had walked out on her husband and infant without explanation. She became heavily involved in mantramic meditation, and sparse communications with home indicated a loss of independent thought, strange philosophical interpretations of life, and an inordinate surrender to the ideologies of the cult. Her speech betrayed incoherent thinking and a difficulty in expressing ideas.

All of that added up to the stark reality that this young woman in her mid-twenties was in grave danger. Unless her family acted now, it might be too late.

Helen's father could not rest. He put every piece of machinery he could think of into operation. He talked with lawyers. He hired private investigators. He flew to cities and townships in which possible sightings of the cult's disciples were reported. He spent a great deal of money and many hours pouring himself into the search for his lost child, relentlessly pursuing the one he loved and whom he longed to see a part of the family once more.

Some weeks after that morning phone call, the stage was set for a rescue. Actually, it was a kidnaping. With the precision of television's make-believe, Helen was snatched by her rescuers in a scene denied all cameras, being on the set of reality. She was taken to another state where she was subjected to the rigors of deprogramming.

That was a painful process; but father and daughter came face to face in a confrontation produced by a father acting against an atrocity that had weighed so heavily upon his mind. Redemption was accomplished in the case of this family. The father paid the price to rescue and free his daughter.

God pined for His children, too. He could never be content to accept His loss and leave it at that. He went searching for His lost sons until that loss was lifted away and replaced with the joy of restoration and reconciliation. Then there was a family reunion!

God the Father Has Redemption on His Mind

God is a redeeming God. That means that He releases slaves by paying a ransom price. Slaves, common in the Roman Empire at the time of Paul's writings, were sometimes bought and then given their freedom. That is why Paul would be understood when he wrote:

> Praise be to the God and Father of our Lord Jesus Christ, who has blessed us in the heavenly realms with every spiritual blessing in Christ. For he chose us in him before the creation of the world to be holy and blameless in his sight. In love he predestined us to be adopted as his sons through Jesus Christ, in accordance with his pleasure and will—to the praise of his glorious grace, which he has freely given us in the One he loves. In him we have redemption through his blood, the forgiveness of sins, in accordance with the riches of God's grace that he lavished on us with all wisdom and understanding (Ephesians 1:3-8).

The Father's divine plan of rescue involved redemption by His Son—an act for which the Father had prepared even before the world began. God has always had His lost children on His mind. That is why He has always had redemption on His mind.

The Need for Redemption

Imagine for a moment that you are a slave. You were not always one, but you are one now. You well remember how you began this life of servitude.

164

You were together with your family, enjoying the love and warmth and mutual care it brought. You had grown accustomed to it. But one day an imposter burst in upon that scene, promising something even better. He said that your father had kept you in his grasp for too long, dominating your life and restricting your freedoms. He promised you autonomy. Your father had often warned you that men might come to try and entice you away by promising a better existence elsewhere; but the imposter's words were so *convincing*! Quickly dismissing the memories of your father's devotion and love, you transferred your loyalties and trust to the imposter.

Within a few days you discovered that the enticer's words were all lies. You found yourself bound to a ruthless master. In that new and stifling setting you grew, married, and had children. They, too, became slaves to your ruthless master, since they were born into that environment. Though you warned them many times not to heed the deceptive and persuasive words of the tyrant, they ignored you as you had your own father. Now they too are obliged to serve the tyrant. Together, you are slaves. Your long bondage has dimmed memories of home and family, and you have virtually given up all hope of freedom.

But today something is about to happen to terminate the bondage. You are to be set free—your father has come! He has found you at last, and he has come to offer everything he owns in an act of love and compassion to purchase your freedom. It has been his greatest desire since the time you departed to see you restored to the joy and beauty and tranquility of the family environment you once boasted. From this very day, you and your children will enjoy freedom from the tyrannical reign of your feared and loathsome taskmaster.

The story of mankind is something like that. Man was made to enjoy the serenity of the Garden of Eden and to walk hand in hand with God. C. Austin Miles attempted to capture the delights of that relationship when he penned the words:

I come to the garden alone
While the dew is still on the roses;
And the voice I hear, falling on my ear,
The Son of God discloses.
And He walks with me and he talks with me,
And He tells me I am His own,
And the joy we share as we tarry there,
None other has ever known.

He speaks, and the sound of His voice,
Is so sweet the birds hush their singing,
And the melody that He gave to me
Within my heart is ringing.
And He walks with me and He talks with me,
And He tells me I am His own,
And the joy we share as we tarry there,
None other has ever known.[1]

But Adam enjoyed that setting only a short while. He could have delighted in it forever—as could each man and woman ever born—if it had not been for Adam's desire to be independent. Like shattered pieces of pottery which once formed a magnificent vessel, man has become a broken relic. The pieces of pottery may be gathered into a heap. They may indicate by their markings that they were once a showpiece of the master potter's work. The original intention of the artist, however, has been lost. The image of the Father in His sons has become sullied. Even their own memory of Him has faded to the point where they deny His existence; He is far from their minds.

The State of the Sinner

Sin obstructs the original design of the world's Artist, God our Father. Mankind is gummed-up in his sin. So much so that it is impossible to break loose.

Have you ever painted a house (or anything else) using oil-based paint? Remember when you reached the end of the day's painting and you realized that you had no turpentine or thinners left? It seemed as if there was more paint on your hands and arms and face than on the brush or in the tin. You were a real mess.

How do you clean up such a disaster area without thinners? Water? Will that help? What happens when you try to wash oil paint off the brush with water? The harder you try, the bigger the mess. The paint not only refuses to dissolve, it rubs in. You end up worse than before. Paint spreads smoothly and evenly all over your hands. Fingers stick together. Frustration builds higher and higher until you are desperate; not only are you all sticky with paint, the stores have closed for the day. The mess remains. Every feeble attempt to clean it up is futile because you cannot displace the oil paint no matter how hard you may try.

Our sin is like that oil paint. Every attempt we make (on our own) to overcome sin and its effects is bound to fail. It's like trying to remove oil paint with water; we just don't have what it takes. The harder we try, the more confirmed in sin we become. We are simply no match for sin's power to sully and spoil our true humanity. It wrecks our family resemblance to the Father.

Sin also obstructs any possible hope for a lost son of God. Imagine you are swimming in the ocean. You are out of your depth and the shore is a few hundred yards away. To make it worse, the sea is full of heavy weed which impedes any progress you might have made. No sooner do you clear one slimy obstruction than there is another before you. Your body grows weary. Finally, you are exhausted. Physical strength drained away, you begin to sink—in despair as well as into the water. Your physical weakness has now become your greatest obstacle.

One final, longing glance toward the shore shows that the weeds have cleared away; but as the waves rise and fall, you realize you have drifted further out to sea. In one final burst of desperate effort, you raise your arms above the water in hopes that one miraculous stroke will sweep you to shore. But alas! Your efforts have all been in vain. You go under for the last time . . . to your death.

Death was inevitable. You were doomed even before your last gasp of breath. You hoped, but there was no hope. All your hope was in yourself, and you simply did not have what it takes. Your hope was no hope at all.

A Lost Son of God Cannot Redeem Himself

When Jonathan Edwards, George Whitefield, and Asahel Nettleton preached to crowds that gathered to hear them in the eighteenth century, listeners developed patterns of response. Men and women were overcome by the Spirit of God and became convincingly assured of their sin, of their "badness." Today the reverse is often true. Modern-day listeners are often so convinced of their "goodness" that it becomes hard for them to be redeemed. In other words, lost sons and daughters of God wander through the wildernesses of life, refusing to acknowledge their lostness, convinced that they can find their way home alone.

Jesus faced that same obstacle. A rich young ruler came to Him on one occasion and asked Him:

> "Good teacher," he asked, "what must I do to inherit eternal life?"
>
> "Why do you call me good?" Jesus answered. "No one is good—except God alone. You know the commandments: 'Do not murder, do not commit adultery, do not steal, do not give false testimony, do not defraud, honor your father and mother.'
>
> "Teacher," he declared, "all these I have kept since I was a boy."
>
> Jesus looked at him and loved him. "One thing you lack," he said. "Go, sell everything you have and give to the poor, and you will have treasure in heaven. Then come, follow me."
>
> At this the man's face fell. He went away sad, because he had great wealth (Mark 10:17-22).

Notice again the young man's question: "What must I do to inherit eternal life?" Jesus' reply was virtually this: "Not the way you thought you could. You have tried to redeem yourself, but you cannot. It is an impossibility because of the true state of your self-centered heart."

The Psalmist confirms the vanity of thinking that self-ransom can cure the greed and self-centeredness of sinful hearts:

No man can redeem the life of another
   or give to God a ransom for him—
the ransom for a life is costly,
   no payment is ever enough
     (Psalm 49:7,8).

The Pharisee who prayed alongside the publican tried to redeem himself by his open piety; but even if this false piety convinced himself, it never convinces the Lord Jesus (see Luke 18:13ff.).

This obstacle of sin and the self-righteousness of lost sons must be eliminated. Sin is the deadliest affront to divine holiness imaginable. So how can it be destroyed?

Nothing but "love divine all loves excelling" can do it. Remember the paint? You need the right cleansing agent to remove it and to free you of its frustrating qualities. The lost and guilty son of God must be cleansed by the Father if that son is to be restored.

The Cost of Redemption

God is the author of life who redeems from death to life, both physical and spiritual. God our Father, who has had the redemption of sons on His mind since eternity, has made the biggest and costliest purchase ever expended. To redeem his lost sons, it cost the Father His only begotten Son, the Lord Jesus Christ, who "gave himself for us to redeem us from all wickedness and to purify for himself a people that are his very own . . . " (Titus 2:14).

Redeeming lost sons cost God His Son. It cost Jesus Christ His life and His fellowship with the Father. Paul told the Galatian church: "Christ redeemed us from the curse of the law by becoming a curse for us, for it is written: 'Cursed is everyone who is hung on a tree'" (Galatians 3:13).

Our Lord willingly endured the shame and curse of the cross when He became your Substitute and mine at Calvary. He endured the transfer of guilt and its consequences. Mark tells us, "For even the Son of Man did not come to be served, but to serve, and to give his life as a ransom for many" (Mark 10:45). C. H. Spurgeon said, "the high street of the gospel runs Cross-wise." This is the high street, the high point of the gospel: that the Son's death on the cross of Calvary purchased the redemption of sons previously lost.

Being a Christian involves a cost. Jesus said, "If anyone would come after me, he must deny himself and take up his cross daily and follow me" (Luke 9:23). Every time the good news of God's grace in Christ Jesus is proclaimed, it should be accompanied by an earnest plea to count the cost involved. There is a cost involved in becoming a Christian and living the Christian life, but there is no price that a man can pay to purchase redemption. You cannot buy it. You cannot earn it. Redemption has been purchased by the shed blood of the Lord Jesus Christ, the Son of God. God Himself has paid the price in giving His only begotten Son. Jesus Christ has given all in His life (His life's blood) as the price. Redemption is free, but it was not cheap.

A lost son is in no position to buy since he is enslaved and impoverished. It is the Redeemer's bloodshedding that avails for the cleansing of the guilty. You have only one option open to you. You can take it as it is freely offered, or you can reject it as foolishness. Do the latter and you reject life. In fact, Jesus Himself said:

> Whoever believes in him [the Son] is not con-
> demned, but whoever does not believe stands
> condemned already because he has not be-
> lieved in the name of God's one and only Son
> (John 3:18).

Those who receive the free offer of redemption in Christ Jesus will enter into true life. They will embark upon a joyous journey through life as a glorious child of God, having realized their true humanity in the tradition of God's people throughout history. There is a cost, though no price to pay. Having redeemed you, God wants His possession. The thing that God wants, above all else, is *you*. He wants your loving service and devotion, your worship and adoration. He wants you to glorify and enjoy Him forever.

The Value of Redemption

Redemption brings sons and daughters into God's family once again, just as He had always intended. They have been restored to the Father as His adopted children—restored to the original relationship in Christ.

What the Father has done in Christ Jesus His Son is to eliminate the hold of guilt over a forgiven child of God. Paul wrote of this:

> Therefore, there is now no condemnation for those who are in Christ Jesus, because through Christ Jesus the law of the Spirit of life set me free from the law of sin and death. For what the law was powerless to do in that it was weakened by the sinful nature, God did by sending his own Son in the likeness of sinful man to be a sin offering (Romans 8:1-3).

God the Father has given His redeemed children redeemed minds, and He expects us to use them throughout our lifetime for the benefit of His kingdom. He expects us to be in the world, though not of it, applying our redeemed minds to matters of moral and political significance in a world intent upon self-destruction. He expects us to struggle with the issues; to look, for example, down the barrels of secular humanistic guns that are spreading the human debris of abortion and infanticide and euthanasia at the feet of the often nonresponsive people of God—and there to demand a ceasefire in the name of holiness and for the cause of mankind.

God our Heavenly Father expects redemption to be worked out to its fullest extent, so that the new life we have in Christ might be authentically applicable in every area of our lives—not simply a topic for theological debate in the ghetto of isolation and introspection where we have no influence upon the world for the causes of heaven and the well-being of men, women, and children.

The Father has rescued His lost sons from that to which they have been enslaved. But where are you today? Are you in the family of God by the grace of His loving actions expressed toward you in Christ Jesus the Son? Perhaps you are still "torn-between-two." You want to be free from sin's enticing power, but you are afraid that the demands of being in the household of God through faith in Christ Jesus will be too burdensome.

If you are thinking those thoughts, it is because there is a spiritual battle going on inside you. J. C. Ryle gave us the reason for your reluctance to take hold of the Father's outstretched hand when he said, "The prince of this world will never allow his captives to be rescued from him without a struggle."

Take hold of the Father's hand. He is strong to rescue—strong to save. He will show you just how wonderful it is to be a part of His family—to have your sins forgiven so that you might reflect the glory of His character in your life. He has the sinner on His mind because the sinner is His lost son, whom He is seeking to save.

> Redeemed—how I love to proclaim it!
> Redeemed by the blood of the Lamb,
> Redeemed through His infinite mercy—
> His child, and forever, I am.[2]

---

1. C. Austin Miles, "In the Garden." Copyright 1912 by Hall-Mack Co. © renewed 1940 by Rodeheaver Co. (a division of Word, Inc.). All rights reserved. International copyright secured. Used by permission.

2. Fanny J. Crosby, "Redeemed" (1820-1915).

CHAPTER
12

IN MY FATHER'S ARMS

Have you ever noticed how arms can so easily convey a message? Waving arms can suggest many different things. They might mean a happy, joyous reunion is about to take place—the prodigal son knew something about that. Waving may become the last, cherished memory of a fond farewell between two friends. But attach fists to the end of those oscillating limbs and you probably have a riot brewing. Waving arms might scribe directions in mid-air; they might reach for the sky when the home team scores a goal; they might signal the exasperation of a confused schoolboy.

But one thing remains certain. Whatever the message in these hieroglyphics of the arms, the one for whom the message is intended will almost invariably understand. I recall one such occasion where the message came through loud and clear.

His secretary had said, "Go on in!" Without hesitation I walked into the office of my elder pastor, knowing that in a matter of moments I would be locked in the clutches of a warm embrace which bubbled, "Welcome! It is wonderful to see you! I love you, my brother; I'm so glad you've come!"

Just twelve months before I had experienced that loving clasp for the first time. My reaction then was very different from that which I felt now. Then it was new to me. Now it was familiar. Then it had caused me an uneasiness, but now I was calm. For this Australian, such overt expressions of genuine, wholesome affection between Christian brothers had always been something that others did—Europeans, Pacific Islanders—but not me. It took leaving my homeland for me to realize just how emotionally reserved we Australians really are. This Australian characteristic (though denied very often) remains obvious to foreigners, and most assuredly to the American observer whose self-giving extrovert tendencies are so readily prompted.

But now my attitude had changed. The very thing that once caused me much apprehension I now anticipated as an obvious sign that I was genuinely loved by my Christian brother. That was the unspoken declaration by my fellow pastor, made with his energetic arms. His openness in putting his arms around me, giving me a fatherly (and brotherly) hug, conveyed the message with a power that a hearty handshake, while fine in itself, could seldom really do.

When I think of God, I immediately think of Him as Father. And that leads me to believe that as my Father, He knows how to embrace me. Moses, who knew what it was like to stand all alone against the stubborn wills of an obstinate people; to feel the pain of disappointment at forfeiting the opportunity to cross the Jordan into Canaan, the promised land; to walk and commune with the living God and then see the truth of His holiness and Person denied in the golden calf—this Moses, who had turned aside to see God and had received revelation of His character at the hand of Yahweh Himself, who had wept over the spiritual state of his charges as they grumbled at the goodness of God in the wilderness, could declare with certainty in his final blessing upon the children of Israel: "The eternal God is your refuge, and underneath are the everlasting arms" (Deuteronomy 33:27).

Moses was convinced. He had experienced it firsthand. He knew it was real. Yahweh, the true God, is Father. Father to the fatherless and the motherless. Father to children, fathers, and mothers alike. The Father, whose love and affection, compassion and mercy, firmness and strength are powerfully known in the midst of embrace. His embrace, that warm clasp of eternal and everlasting arms that sustains and keeps His children in the most trying of circumstances.

This was not the testimony of a novice. Moses was no rookie. He had walked with God for many years and had seen a special promise fulfilled many times over. Called by God to stand against Pharaoh, Moses had protested, "Who am I, that I should go to Pharaoh and bring the Israelites out of Egypt?" (Exodus 3:11).

But God promised, "Certainly I will be with you" (v. 12 NASB).

The promise was made—and kept. Not only in Pharaoh's case, but when crossing the Red Sea, when the people mutinied, when food was needed and water scarce. Kept in the war against Amalek and when the people turned to idolatry at the foot of Mount Sinai. Through grumbling and disbelief, struggles and torment of mind, this God-appointed leader of Israel endured throughout the course of his life; and one thing typified Moses' relationship with his heavenly Father. It was intimate.

We are told, "The LORD would speak to Moses face to face, as a man speaks with his friend" (Exodus 33:11).

Can you think of a more beautiful relationship—a more humbling or glorious experience? The living God communing with a man! The Creator in touch with the creature! The Holy God, whose eyes are too pure to look upon sin and allow it to pass by unchallenged, speaking with a sinful Hebrew! And not only speaking with him, but making promises to him, befriending him. Incredible!

In our more incredulous moments we want to dismiss such a suggestion as fantasy. How could it ever be? What are we that we could believe such a thing! Yet Moses testifies to its authenticity. He states unequivocally:

> "There is no one like the God of Jeshurun,
>   who rides on the heavens to help you
>   and on the clouds in his majesty.

The eternal God is your refuge,
and underneath are the everlasting arms.
(Deuteronomy 33:26,27)

He knew the warmth of the Father's embrace!

When My Arms Are Weak, His Arms Are Strong

Even when my arms seem strong, His are stronger. When everything is going so smoothly that I think I'm self-sufficient, I fail to see the strength of my heavenly Father's arms. I am deluded into thinking that I am invincible.

Not so when I am crushed. Not so when the weight of sorrow or sudden illness, depression or debilitating news descends upon me like the dark clouds of a summer storm that mount up late in the afternoon across a tropical sky. Then I am weak, and I know it.

One morning, while praying for a friend who had been suffering from a mysterious ailment for some time, I came across a Psalm which so challenged my heart that I phoned her to share the Psalmist's thoughts of God. When my friend answered, she gave the latest prognosis: It might mean surgery on the brain. But this delightfully optimistic lady told me, "Well, it wasn't exactly the choice I had in mind, but the Lord knows all about it." Then she proceeded to read to me the passage that had so helped her earlier in the day when she was beginning to compare herself with healthy friends and question why God would put her through this particular hardship:

Consider what God has done:
Who can straighten
what he has made crooked?
(Ecclesiastes 7:13)

Why, of course—who but God Himself? God the Father, who has made each of us according to His own purposes, who has held me in His hand and encompassed me with His arms, knows all about me! The Psalmist writes:

For you created my inmost being;
you knit me together in my mother's womb.

I praise you because I am fearfully and wonder-
fully made;
your works are wonderful,
I know that full well.
My frame was not hidden from you
when I was made in the secret place.
When I was woven together in the depths of the
earth,
your eyes saw my unformed body.
All the days ordained for me
were written in your book
before one of them came to be.
(Psalm 139:13-16).

Whose earthly father could ever boast of knowing that much about his child? I am so glad my Heavenly Father knows me that intimately. It gives me the kind of confidence that I need when my fears are threatening to mount.

Such knowledge brings a quiet peace to bear upon my sense of uncertainty—when the future of my health is clouded, or the waiting becomes unbearable—to allay those fears which otherwise may absorb my energy with an all-consuming passion.

Father, Put Your Arms Around Me, Please

I entered her hospital room and peered around the end of a dividing wall. There she was. Still. Thoughtful. Waiting the long wait. Too sick to do anything and without the emotional energy to try. Even worry was interrupted by waves of disorientation brought on by a medication which numbed some of the pain. Her tired lids lifted and her eyes met those of a pastor who never really knows what to say during moments of anxiety in the elevator or hospital corridor.

A smile gently spread across her young face, belying the ordeal she had just endured. As it faded, I could tell the pain remained.

"How are you?" I asked, as if that wasn't already obvious.

177

"I'm doing okay," she said, looking up at me in expectation of what this visitor might say to encourage her in the midst of her worst fears.

"How is Brent?" I inquired, uncertain of what may have transpired since the last bulletin on his progress.

"Every hour passed is another milestone," she said. "We're just waiting."

Maren's baby had been taken by Caesarean section at twenty-five weeks. Now mother and child played a waiting game in separate sections of the hospital wing. Little Brent, all one pound, three ounces of precious human flesh, palpitated to the rhythm of another "mother's" heartbeat—the respirator.

He was unconscious of his battle with life. Unaware of the aching which constantly nagged at his real mother's heart. Oblivious? Perhaps. *But alive.* Tiny, but ever so significant. Seemingly at the mercy of man-made machinery, but all the while in the arms of his Heavenly Father—minute by each long, drawn-out minute.

Hope against hope. I could read it in her eyes. We exchanged a few thoughts. We read encouraging words from the Psalms and from Paul's letter to the Philippian church. I reached out for her hand and placed it between my own hands. Looking up, I began to speak, conscious by now that her eyes were floating in a warm sea of liquid anxiety we call tears.

"Maren. I want you to remember right now that God is your loving Father. I want you to realize that His strong, caring arms are around you right at this moment. You are His precious child, His treasured possession, and He knows everything that you are experiencing at this very minute."

Her lips trembled apart to reveal mental assent. It was a faint smile.

"As your Heavenly Father, He cares more for you in this moment than you could ever know, regardless of future events. One more thing. Brent is His child, too. He cares about him in the same way He cares about you. He loves you both. And He is the most faithful of all fathers. Trust Him."

It reminds me so much of the times one of our girls has fallen and hurt herself, or taken sick, or come home from school in tears as the result of something a thoughtless peer has said.

"Daddy, put your arms around me, please."

When we ache for one another, when we long to help but feel so helpless, our prayer so often becomes:

"Father, put your arms around her, please."

But how long do arms have to be? Little Brent continued to eke out his days in the sterilized substitute for his mom's internal environment. Tubes came out of his nose, out of his chest, from his stomach. This tiny little doll with moving hands and feet had a greater control over graphs on machines than I ever did in my math classes. I stood looking at this precious little person, amazed at the completeness of his features, despite his size.

And what a size.

His arms were so tiny that Jeff, his father, could take his wedding ring, pass it over the infant's hand and right up the length of his little arm. Yet with those miniature arms he expressed the fighting spirit God had given him to help cope against all obstacles. He would pull at the tubes and kick his legs off the mat like a wrestler grappling with an opponent.

That is just about how strong Brent's parents felt throughout their long journey, waiting for the day when their son would really be theirs . . . at home . . . in their arms in the morning and again at night. They felt as helpless as the baby himself, reliant upon doctors and nurses in a way little different from the child. But in spite of apparent obstacles, in spite of what seemed to be insurmountable complications, a quiet confidence beat in their hearts. They knew their heavenly Father and they knew He cared.

They knew the embrace of the Father in the midst of personal weakness, and could acknowledge with the Psalmist concerning Him, "Your arm is endued with power; your hand is strong, your right hand exalted" (Psalm 89:13). Both Jeff and Maren have realized in practice that it is at our weakest point that we come to appreciate how strong our loving heavenly Father's grace really is—sufficient for every need.

The day came when Maren held her arms out for the first time, took Brent into them, and cradled his petite body next to her own. This was the moment she had been waiting for. Mother and child together, enjoying the sensations normally shared at the time of birth, but to this point denied both mother and son. The joy, however, was short-lived. Brent's sensitivity to a foreign environment—new touch, different smells, feelings of insecurity—sent his little heart fluttering, his breathing erratic and the graph on the machine haywire. He was so agitated that it took some time before his breathing became steady (likewise for mother).

Within a few weeks, and at the increased weight of two pounds, Brent was ready for a second try. So was Maren! This time it was different. There was no sense of agitation, no short breath, no scares for Mom or nurses. In fact, Brent enjoyed every minute of it. Resting in his mother's arms, still attached to his machine like an astronaut to the mother ship during a space walk, Brent relaxed. Actually, he *trusted*. He allowed himself to be cradled in the security of his mother's arms. There he was at peace.

Little Brent proved to be quite a teacher. Think about it for a moment. That is so like us with our Heavenly Father. In the midst of uncertainty, when the walls are tumbling down around our ears, when we are at our lowest emotional and physical ebb, He whispers in our ears, "Trust Me." He takes us in His arms and seeks to embrace us in the midst of our anxiety—but we become agitated and fitful. Wanting to feel our own base of security, we kick our legs and wave our arms; we develop faulty breathing and utter cries of despair until He puts us down where we again try to make it on our own. And as long as we walk the tightrope alone, as long as we kick against His overtures and fatherly advances, we continue to miss the joys of His secure embrace and the peace which passes all understanding.

When finally we rest in His arms, regardless of what we may have sensed at first to be an insecure position—a shaky circumstance, fears about the future—we will know peace. His peace. A peace which is the fruit of trusting.

> Father-like He tends and spares us,
> Well our feeble frame He knows,
> In His arms He gently bears us,
> Rescues us from all our foes.[1]

---

1. H. F. Lyte, "Praise, My Soul, the King of Heaven" (1783-1847).

13

BY MY FATHER'S GRACE, IN GLORY

A lady once asked John Wesley, "Supposing that you knew you were to die at twelve o'clock tomorrow night, how would you spend the intervening time?"

"How, madam?" he replied. "Why, just as I intend to spend it now. I should preach this evening at Gloucester, and again at five tomorrow morning; after that I should ride to Tewkesbury, preach in the afternoon, and meet the societies in the evening. I should then retire to my friend's house, who expects to entertain me, talk and pray with the family as usual, retire to my room at ten o'clock, commend myself to my heavenly Father, lie down to rest and wake up in glory."[1]

It's old fashioned to speak of heaven as *Glory*! But then, Wesley was "old fashioned."

It's old fashioned for some people to even speak of heaven at all. God is considered old fashioned. So too is church.

Christianity, in the view of many, is simply too outmoded to be of any use in a modern world where the silicon chip reigns. It's just old fashioned talk.

A grandfather clock is considered an old-timer! And Christianity is considered an old-timer's religion. But is it?

Our youngest daughter recently burst through the kitchen door of our apartment, right into the middle of my wife and me giving each other a hug and a kiss. She stopped in her tracks, looked up, shrugged her shoulders, and walked off, saying, "Oh, that's just what they were doing upstairs on the TV—it was an old-fashioned movie!" My wife and I together chimed in happily, "Well, we're just old fashioned!"

When it comes to *life*, and when it comes to *death*, when it boils right down to my taking that final breath on this earth, if believing what I read in the Bible is old fashioned, then I'm so happy to be old fashioned!

In our Lord's priestly prayer to the Father, three things highlight the truth that every Christian will one day be with the Father in Glory, in heaven. Jesus asked the Father to

- Preserve Christians, His followers, from the evil one (John 17:15).
- Sanctify believers to make them holy (John 17:17).
- Unify His children—to make them one in purpose (John 17:21-23).

But in verse 24, the Lord Jesus' request is for their participation in something. That something is participation in His glory. Jesus prayed:

Father, I want those you have given me to be with me where I am, and to see my glory, the glory you have given me because you loved me before the creation of the world.

Jesus Desires His Own

First, we see that the Lord Jesus has a glorious desire for us. He *desires* those whom the Father has given Him on earth. He wills to have them. He longs for them. With His love He has sought me. With His blood He has bought me. And now—He longs for the day when He will say to each one of God's children whose salvation was entrusted into His hands, "Come, you who are blessed by my Father; take your inheritance, the kingdom prepared for you since the creation of the world" (Matthew 25:34).

He longs for the inheritance which He purchased with His blood. He longs for the day when the whole of God's redeemed family is brought together at the Father's beckoning, to surround His throne in heaven and to unite in praise and worship at God's feet. Little wonder that the Psalmist could write, "Precious in the sight of the LORD is the death of his saints" (Psalm 116:15).

Every time a saint goes home to be at the Father's side, the Lord Jesus receives part of the answer to His prayer. Dear friend, God views death so differently from us!

At the graveside of Lazarus, Jesus our Lord saw the sting of death. He displayed in no uncertain terms that He was on a crusade against the very sting that kept men and women in its grip—against that tyrannical oppressor of human nature called *sin* which brandished death as its ultimate weapon. He went out and destroyed its tyranny at the cross of Calvary. He destroyed the obscenity of human helplessness in the face of sin, a victory declared in the resurrection Paul wrote about:

> The sting of death is sin, and the power of sin is the law. But thanks be to God! He gives us the victory through our Lord Jesus Christ (1 Corinthians 15:56).
> Where, O death, is your victory? Where, O death, is your sting? (1 Corinthians 15:55).

God views it so differently from us.

Jesus turned death into life. John Newton understood that. In his dying moments, Newton said, "I am still in the land of the dying; soon I will be in the land of the living!"

The one whose life was poured out in death to bring life to a dying world longs to have His inheritance. And thus He prayed to the Father, "Father, it is my will . . . I desire them . . ." Why? Because, as Solomon wrote, "I belong to my lover, and his desire is for me" (Song of Solomon 7:10).

Jesus Has Something for Us

Second, we notice that the Lord Jesus has a glorious position for us. C. H. Spurgeon said of this priestly prayer, "At a single stride, His prayer sets foot in glory."[2]

Will you notice Jesus' prayer? The way He speaks, He might well be in heaven already. He might well have already gained what He is asking for in His prayer.

That is a model prayer—to so cease from the cares, the battles, the agonies of the world—to rise in such fellowship with God as to think and speak in prayer as if we already stood in the Father's presence, the answer at our side.

We do well to learn from Jesus' prayer, to approach our heavenly Father with the confidence of His adopted children.

> Father, I want those you have given me to be with
> me where I am . . .

At His side! In the Father's presence! There is going to be a homecoming!

When we left Australia—a beautiful land where the sun beats back the rain, and where, if the rain keeps up, it never comes down—we waved goodbye to family. Personal family and church family. In the back of our minds was the thought, "There will be a homecoming—when the waves of goodbye will become waves of hello, when the tears of sadness at leaving will change into tears of joy at reunion; when we will stand together again, side by side."

There is going to be a homecoming! There is going to be a family gathering, a reunion of God's children with the Father and with the Son. There can be no better place for a reunion than in the Father's house. What can be more right than God's children being at home with the Father?

That reunion comes sooner for some than for others. Even when we are parted from loved ones there is an attraction which draws our affections to them—whether separated by a state or a sea. The same is true of our Lord Jesus. He holds the heavenly magnet in His hand which attracts us to Him. Some return sooner than we might wish. As Spurgeon put it, "our ripe saints go home, because the Beloved is come into His garden to gather lilies."[3] And it is so hard for us to let them go. But we must. The very goal of our existence is to dwell in the Father's presence. The sorrow of our human natures, the thing that plagues our lives, is that we live apart from the Father and His home.

Sin has caused us, in time past, to play the prodigal.

We have returned only through repentance and faith, by trusting in Jesus Christ as Savior and Lord.

Jesus came from the Father with one thing in mind—to lead us back to the Father again! We must let our loved ones go to Him.

The Pied Piper played a tune which captured the exclusive attention of every child in the land. When they heard his tune, they gave attention to it to the exclusion of all other voices. When Jesus Christ the Lord, the Son of the living God, calls His children home, they hear the music of His beckoning to the exclusion of all other voices.

We call out, "Come back! Don't leave us yet! It's too soon! We have things to discuss! There's something I needed to say! Plans to make! A future to accomplish!" But they cannot hear! They are tuned to a different wave length, tuned to the frequency of the Father's call. They are enroute to the Father's house where the Lord Jesus has prepared a place for them. There they behold the Son's glory. There they reflect the Father's glory. There they glorify God and there they will enjoy Him forever. Knowing that, we do not complain at our loss!

When Jesus was about to leave, His disciples expressed their natural disappointment at His words, "I go . . . "

Jesus spoke to them in this way:

> You heard me say, "I am going away and I am
> coming back to you." If you loved me, you would
> be glad that I am going to the Father (John
> 14:28).

Our Lord's will is that His loved ones be with Him, at His side, with the Father. It is His will that the whole Church on earth be with Him, that each and all be with Him to see His glory. There is no distinction. He wants all the saints with Himself.

Notice the nearness of the saints with Christ in glory. What fellowship could be sweeter? Who would wish to detain a Christian loved one and friend from such companionship? Companionship with the Savior! To be literally with Jesus Christ the Lord. J. C. Ryle wrote, "It is company and not place which makes up happiness." I don't think we could imagine either better company or better place than to be with the Lord Jesus in heaven.

Are we wrong to weep? No! Certainly not. To weep is normal and healthy. But when we weep, we weep for ourselves. Their companionship is with the Altogether Lovely One. Their place with the Lord Jesus in the Father's presence seals their delight. When we think of that, our tears soften and a smile breaks forth. Comfort yourselves in the twin thoughts of their joy in Christ and Christ's joy in them.

Jesus Has a Surprise for Us

Third, we notice that the Lord Jesus has a glorious surprise for us:

> Father, I want those you have given me to be with
> me where I am, and to see my glory, the glory you
> have given me because you loved me before the
> creation of the world (John 17:24).

Do you like surprises? The surprise our Lord has in store for God's children is much more exciting than we may have ever anticipated.

The day we received word that our family would be coming to Portland, a lady in our church family came over to our house and offered to look after the children. She packed Margo and me off to see two films—a sort of celebration at the thought of our adventure. When I tell you what she packed us off to see, you may wonder what her motive was!

The first film was an Australian work, *The Man from Snowy River*. The second showed Mt. St. Helens's eruption. Like all shots of the mountain taken with telescopic lenses, Portland appeared totally dwarfed by this massive, nasty, flame-spitting volcano.

It made quite an impression on us—watching a cubic mile of mountain spit into the air by gargantuan explosions of the sort we could hardly imagine. The worst blast we had ever seen was a ginger-beer bottle explosion in the kitchen cupboard! The evening had its effect: Some of the most beautiful of Australia's countryside, double-billed with the most frightening-looking mountain we had ever seen.

Let me ask you—where would you want to be, in our shoes?

We went home, wondering whether we ought to cancel our plans to live in Portland. Something happened, however, to change all that, to allay the fears and replace them with breathtaking delight.

We arrived in Portland to sunshine and blue skies. We visited the beautiful, snowcapped Mount Hood. We could look out and see just how far Mt. St. Helens really was from Portland. And we were delighted! What a surprise! It was all so beautiful. We had never seen anything like it before!

Now we want our family and friends to come! We want them to come and see the Cascades as much as we want to take our American friends back to Australia to show them beautiful blue surf that is so warm that you can actually swim in it! Hillsides reaching down to the sea, covered in banana and pineapple plantations. People whose accents would fascinate you! We just know our "stateside" friends would love it there.

That is exactly how Jesus feels about the heavenly home He is preparing for us. There is so much more than we might expect. He prayed, "Father, I want them to be where I am, seeing my glory. They would love it!" We would see Him in a light in which we have not seen Him before. We would see the true glory of the One who came forth from the Father full of grace and truth! We will be restored to the Father.

As those created out of His glory, for His glory, to be reflectors of His glory, we had fallen short of what God intended for His children. We needed to be restored to the Father again.

In heaven we will be restored to the glorious status designed by the Father. We will know the glory of our Savior. We will appreciate the words of the Psalmist:

> When I consider your heavens,
>   the work of your fingers,
>   the moon and the stars,
>   which you have set in place,

what is man that you are mindful of him,
    the son of man that you care for him?
You made him a little lower than the heavenly
    beings
      and crowned him with glory and honor.
        (Psalm 8:3-5)

We will see God's glory! What will it produce in us? Moses saw something of God's glory: "Now show me your glory" (Exodus 33:18). What was the result? Moses made haste to bow low toward the earth to worship. Isaiah saw something of God's glory (Isaiah 6), and he was brought to worship. Stephen, full of the Holy Spirit, gazed intently into heaven from the vantage point granted him by God in his final minutes, and saw the glory of God with Jesus standing at the right hand of His Father (Acts 7:55). John gives us a picture in Revelation:

> Each of the four living creatures had six wings and was covered with eyes all around, even under his wings. Day and night they never stop saying:
> > "Holy, holy, holy
> > is the Lord God Almighty,
> > who was, and is, and is to come."
> Whenever the living creatures give glory, honor and thanks to him who sits on the throne and who lives for ever and ever, the twenty-four elders fall down before him who sits on the throne, and worship him who lives for ever and ever. They lay their crowns before the throne and say:
> > You are worthy, our Lord and God,
> >   to receive glory and honor and power,
> > for you created all things,
> >   and by your will they were created
> >   and have their being."
> > (Revelation 4:8-11)

Created to worship God, on that day we will know its true meaning. Created to love the Father, we will know His smile. The time of preparation will have ended—and we will be at home:

> —with the Father
> —with the family
> —*forever.*

Conclusion

When Martin Luther accidentally discovered a complete Bible chained to the wall in the library at Efurt, it amazed and thrilled him. But Dr. Usinger, one of his teachers, discouraged his interest in it.

"Ah, brother Martin, what is there in the Bible?" he asked. "It is better to read the books of the ancient doctors. They have sucked the honey of the truth. The Bible is the cause of all the troubles in the church."

But it *is* to the Bible that we turn as children of God to confidently find gracious words of comfort for life and eternity.

There is nothing exciting about passing into eternity for anyone who will not go through the curtain hand-in-hand with Jesus Christ as their Savior and Lord. Are you "old fashioned" enough to delight in Jesus' prayer:

> Father, I want those you have given me to be with me where I am, and to see my glory, the glory you have given me because you loved me before the creation of the world (John 17:24).

To be at the Father's side is to be where the Son of God prayed that God's children would be—together, with the Son, at the Father's side. That took an act of grace . . . but then, we have a gracious Father.

The ultimate unveiling of sonship will be in glory. The apostle Paul stated it so profoundly:

> I consider that our present sufferings are not worth comparing with the glory that will be revealed in us. The creation waits in eager expectation for the sons of God to be revealed (Romans 8:18-19).

Father, we adore you.

1. Arthur T. Pierson, *Seed Thoughts* (New York: Funk & Wagnalls, 1900), p. 94.

2. Charles H. Spurgeon, *Metropolitan Tabernacle Pulpit*, vol. 32 (London: Passmore and Alabaster, 1886), p. 169.

3. Ibid., p. 171.

Selected Bibliography

Bingham, Geoffrey C. *Father! My Father!* Adelaide: New Creation Publications, 1977.

Buchanan, J. *The Doctrine of Justification.* London: Banner of Truth Trust, 1961.

Forsyth, P. T. *God the Holy Father.* London: Independent Press, 1957.

Lidgett, J. S. *The Fatherhood of God.* Edinburgh: T & T Clark, 1902.

Packer, J. I. *Knowing God.* Downers Grove, Ill.: InterVarsity Press, 1973.

Ridderbos, Herman. *The Coming of the Kingdom.* Philadelphia: The Presbyterian and Reformed Publishing Co., 1962.

Shaw, J. M. *The Christian Gospel of the Fatherhood of God.* London: Hodder, 1924.

Smail, Thomas A. *The Forgotten Father.* Grand Rapids: William B. Eerdmans Publishing Co., 1980.

Thielicke, Helmut. *The Waiting Father.* New York: Harper and Row Publishers, 1959.

Subject Index

SUBJECT INDEX